A Chill Guide

to the Land of

K

OksusuPie™

A Chill Guide to the Land of K

Written and illustrated by **Ihm Minyong**
Designed by **UrbanSnail**
Special thanks to **Eunha Ranft**,
for the keen editorial eye and endless patience.

IngramSpark Edition
ISBN 978-1-955878-01-2

First edition published in November 2025
Published by **OksusuPie**™
An imprint of BokeeCo

oksusupie.kr

▌Style Notes:

Romanization
Use Revised Romanization; no hyphens in common nouns
- e.g., *jjimjilbang*, Gyeongseong

  ### -Note-
  All romanization follows the Principles of Loanword Orthography established by the National Institute of Korean Language.

People's Names
Romanization only; hyphenate given-name syllables
- e.g., Bong Jun-ho, Lee Byung-hun

K-terms
Romanize, then co-list Korean at first mention
- e.g., *oktapbang* 옥탑방 (rooftop room)

Places
Co-list Hangul after English for place names
- e.g., Seoul 서울, Busan 부산

Contents' Titles
English first, then Hangeul
- e.g., Parasite 기생충

In the main text, use English titles only.

Articles & Sorting (Appendix only)
In the Appendix, ignore "The" for alphabetizing and place them at the end
- e.g., School Nurse Files, The

^A Chill Guide

to the Land of K

● Greetings from Korea

We, Koreans often describe our country as Dynamic Korea. After the devastation of the Korean War in the 1950s, the country rebuilt itself at startling speed. Not just recovered - it advanced at a pace few could imagine. Generations of change were compressed into several decades.

In Seoul, you might sit in a palace courtyard that looks like something out of the zombie drama Kingdom, and look up at a skyline of glass. Towers stretch along the streets like a vertical forest. A few blocks away, narrow alleys are lined with old taverns and shops that haven't changed in nearly a century.

Korean culture mixes opposites - past and future, tradition and tech. The result is something distinct, and very much alive.

This book offers an intimate loop around Korea. Not just the big sights, but the small things. The kind you notice when you take a side street - a story, a sound, a glimpse of something real, folded into the everyday.

Through K-content: dramas, films, food, webtoons, K-Pop and more, we invite you to see not only what Korea looks like, but how it feels. We hope you find a few of those moments here.

This book reflects personal impressions of Korean culture, not academic conclusions. Readers may see things differently - and that's part of the story, too.

Cheers, Minyong

Myojak-do (Cats and Sparrows, partial view)
By Byeon Sang-byeok, 18th century

● **Meet** Your Guide, **Susu**

Hi, I'm Susu — 37th-generation Korean domestic shorthair.

Rumor has it one of my ancestors showed up in a 18th-century folk painting. I haven't fact-checked it... but it sounds fancy, so I'll go with it.

Describe myself? Drama lover. Big Buldak noodle fan. But Horrors? No thanks.

I totally admire Hochi from Buldak and Director Bong from Parasite... but honestly, I hope I never meet either of them in person.

When it comes to K-dramas, I never know when to stop. And yes, I love boxes - what cat doesn't? Obviously.

Open mine one by one as you go. You'll find little stories tucked inside. I'll be sneaking through alleys and corners, whispering K-facts along the way.

"**Stay Tuned.**"

Language

K

K-Pop

Codes

Creatures

Styles

Foods

Destinations

History

Fast Facts

Follow Me!

K ALLEY

Spotting K

1 Spotting Korea on the Globe

Nestled in Northeast Asia, Korea sits close to China, Russia, and Japan, each playing a part in its unique geography and history. The country stretches out from the eastern edge of the Asian continent, forming a peninsula - not unlike Italy in shape, though you'll have to look a lot farther east to find it. But Korea's story isn't quite so simple.

Since the Korean War armistice in 1953, the peninsula has been divided into two with very different political systems. Because of this split, South Korea, located in the southern part of the peninsula, is often described as "island-like" - effectively cut off from the mainland by the border with North Korea.

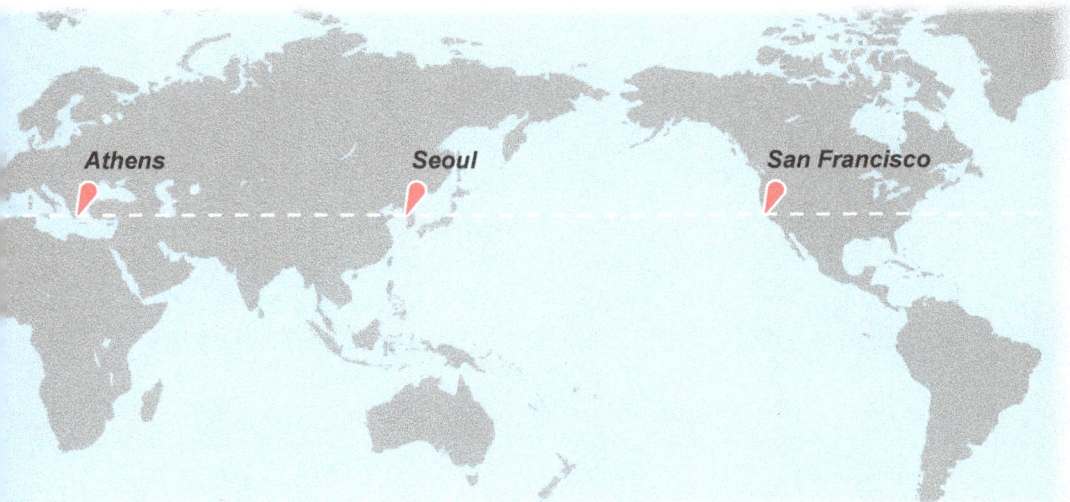

Athens   Seoul   San Francisco

In terms of latitude, South Korea lines up with some familiar places: London, Madrid, Istanbul, and Washington, D.C. all sit at roughly the same distance from the equator - though the climate and culture, of course, tell a very different story.

South Korea experiences distinct four seasons, with longer summers and winters, and spring and autumn being well-defined. The annual average temperature is 12.5°C (54.5°F), with peak summer temperatures reaching over 40°C (104°F) and winter lows dropping to almost -20°C (-4°F), creating a rollercoaster-like weather pattern. Naturally, Koreans are always fully geared up to handle the changing weather. *(Korea Meteorological Administration)*

Susu's Box

Ah-ah "아아" in Winter: Korea's Iced Obsession

In Korea, iced Americano isn't just a summer drink - it's a year-round lingo for caffeine : a "caffeine IV drip"

The nickname *Ah-ah* "아아" (short for ice Americano 아이스 아메리카노) is so common that it's casually used in cafés and group chats, often contrasted with *Tteu-ah* "뜨아" (hot Americano).

On a scorching summer day, people cool down with an *Ah-ah* "아아" after a steaming-hot, spicy meal. And in the middle of winter, it's not unusual to see office workers sipping iced coffee with gloved hands, bundled up in long black puffers. Some say the iced version isn't just about temperature - it's easier to drink quickly, so you can get your caffeine fix without waiting for it to cool. Whether strong and bold or light and sweet, *Ah-ah* "아아" is more than just a drink - it's a ritual woven into daily Korean life.

South Korea is a peninsula surrounded by the sea on three sides, and nearly 70% of its land is mountainous. That means there aren't many flat areas to live on - so the places where people can live have been developed intensively, leading to one of the highest population densities in the world. *(Korea Statistical Information Service, KOSIS, 2024)*

And surprisingly, Seoul 서울 is actually not that far from Pyongyang, the capital of North Korea - because Seoul itself is located quite far north within South Korea. You could technically drive to Pyongyang in about three hours, if that were ever possible. On a clear day, you can even catch a glimpse of North Korean landscapes from Seoul's tallest buildings. It's also so close to the border that Panmunjom, the truce village in the DMZ, is less than an hour away by car.

▌JSA (Joint Security Area) 2000 • movie

Directed by Park Chan-wook, this film features the young faces of Song Kang-ho and Lee Byung-hun. Set in the Demilitarized Zone, it follows soldiers from both North and South Korea who secretly share a bond of friendship. Their clandestine meetings are eventually discovered, leading to a tragic and irreversible turn of events. Both tense and deeply human, the film remains one of the most poignant depictions of Korea's divided reality.

D.P. 1,2 (Deserter Pursuit) 2021, 2023 • drama

Starring Jung Hae-in, Son Suk-ku, and Koo Kyo-hwan, DP centers on a special military unit tasked with capturing deserters - young men who flee conscription for reasons of their own. The series sheds light on the harsh realities of barracks life, particularly the abuses and bullying once prevalent in the system. While these issues have eased in recent years, the show struck a nerve for its candid look at military service - an obligation that still touches nearly every Korean family.

Now, let's zoom in and take a closer look at Korea through the numbers. Here's a quick snapshot of some key figures that define the country and its people.

2 Fast Facts & Hidden Surprises

Before diving into all things K - stories, trends, and trivia - here's a quick snapshot of the country itself. Numbers can't explain everything - but in Korea, even statistics have a story to tell.

- **Coordinates:** 33°– 43° N, 124°–132° E
  (Ministry of Land, Infrastructure and Transport, 2024)

- **Size-wise:** Portugal • Hungary • Indiana, USA

- **Total area:** 100,460 km² *(KOSIS, 2024)*

- **Time Zone:** KST (Korea Standard Time) / UTC +9

- **Population & Density**
  - **Total population: 51.7 million**
    Nearly half the population lives in the capital region, creating a vertical sprawl around Seoul.
  - **Seoul Metropolitan Area population: 23.0 million**
    Nearly 45% of South Koreans live on just 11% of the country's land.
  - **National population density: 515.4 people per km²**
  - **Seoul population density: 15,506 people per km²**
    ≈ 30× national average
    ≈ 1.6× New York (approximately 10,195 people/km²)
    (Korean Statistical Information Service, 2024)

- **Foreign residents:** Nearly 3 million (**5.7%**)
  (Ministry of Justice, Immigration Office, 2024)

- **Top nationalities** • Chinese 36% • Thai 7% • American 6%
  • Vietnamese 2% • Uzbek 4%

- **Ethnic composition:**
  Korea is one of the world's most ethnically homogeneous nations - a result of centuries of settled life on a peninsula with little largescale migration.

- **Official Language:** Korean (*hangugeo* 한국어)

- **Per capita GDP:** $35,570 *(KOSIS, 2024)*
- **Currency:** KRW (Korean Won 원)

- **Administrative divisions:** *(Ministry of the Interior and Safety, 2023)*
  1 Special City (Seoul 서울, the capital)
  6 Metropolitan Cities
  1 Special Self-Governing City (Sejong 세종, administrative capital)
  6 Provinces
  3 Special Self-Governing Provinces (including Jeju 제주)

- **Political system:** *(Doopedia, 2024)*
  Presidential system by direct election 5-year single term
  Three branches: Executive, Legislative (National Assembly), Judiciary

- **College enrollment rate: 75%** *(KEDI, 2024)*
- **Average sleep time: 6h 27m** *(IKEA Sleep Uncovered, 2024)*
- **Streaming subscription rate:** 79.2%
  Average user subscribes to 2.3 services *(Chosun Ilbo, 2024)*

- **Food delivery app usage frequency:** *(ETNews, 2024)*
  1–3 times per month: 36.5%
  1–2 times per week: 30.6%
  More frequent among younger users
  (20s: use 3–4 times per week 15.2%)

  Main reason for use :
  "Too lazy to go out" — 68.6%

  Most ordered food :
  Fried chicken — 47.5%

NOTE: All figures are rounded for clarity.

National
Flag, Flower & Martial Arts

Taegeukgi 태극기

The flag of Korea features a red-and-blue taegeuk circle at the center, symbolizing the harmony and balance between yin (blue) and yang (red) with four black trigrams.

The trigrams are arranged clockwise from the upper left: Geon (Heaven), Gam (Water), Gon (Earth), and Li (Fire). Together, these symbols express the unity of opposites and the natural order of the universe.

Beyond its political role as a national emblem, the Taegeukgi's symbols are widely incorporated into art, fashion, and contemporary design, reflecting Korea's cultural identity.

Mugunghwa 무궁화
(Hibiscus syriacus)

Called the "flower that never fades," Mugunghwa symbolizes resilience and endurance. Its name, *mugung* 무궁, means eternity - reflecting Korea's spirit of perseverance

Taekwondo 태권도

A Korean martial art with origins in the martial ethos of the Three Kingdoms era, Taekwondo emphasizes speed, agility, and dynamic kicks.

Yet over time, it has transcended its combative roots to become a discipline of self-cultivation - embodying respect, restraint, and the pursuit of harmony between mind and body.

In modern Korea, taekwondo studios serve not only as training grounds for martial arts but also as a second home for children.

Kids practice taekwondo, work toward belt promotions, celebrate birthdays, learn basic manners, do their homework, eat pizza, and often get a ride home after a full day at the studio.

Susu's Box

Homes of K

Most Koreans live in apartments - not the romantic kind with balconies and garden chairs, but high-rise complexes that dominate the skyline. With about 70% of the country covered in mountains, cities go vertical by necessity. Over half the population lives in apartments, while the rest are spread across detached houses and small multi-unit buildings - usually called villas 빌라 or *dasaedae* 다세대 (multi-unit house). Some of these even come with *oktapbang* 옥탑방 (rooftop rooms) or *banjiha* 반지하 (semi-basements).

Shoes off at the door, *ondol* 온돌 (heated floors), and high-rise living - these are the basics of Korean homes. But K-dramas often reveal more: the semi-basements of 'Parasite', the rooftop rooms of 'Stranger', or the glamorous penthouses of 'My Love from the Star' or the luxury dorms of Huntrix - each space doubling as a stage for Korea's dramas, both on screen and off.

Hanok 한옥(traditional Korean houses), looks very different, yet followed the same logic: adapt to nature. Built with wood, they featured *maru* 마루(raised wooden floors), for cool summers and ondol for warm winters. Curved eaves let in the winter sun while blocking rain. Layouts embraced an inner courtyard, bringing sunlight and air into the home.

And because the floor itself is the warmest seat in the house, sofas often work less as couches and more as simple backrests - something you could spot in many homes today.

Traditional **Furniture**

Soban 소반

A small portable dining table used to hold dishes, crafted in a variety of tabletop and leg designs.

Sabangtakja 사방탁자

A simple wooden table with four legs and flat shelves, often found in a scholar's room. It was used to hold books or display ornamental objects. Its open structure conveyed a sense of lightness, harmonizing with other low furnishings.

Seoan 서안

A small traditional low desk designed for reading or writing while seated on the floor.

Where
Drama Characters Reside

Banjiha 반지하 (Semi-basement)

Parasite 기생충 2019 • movie

Kitaek's family (Song Kang-ho) lives in a semi-basement, forever hunting for Wi-Fi. Their home floods in the rainy season, a vivid symbol of social status. Recently, Seoul has begun regulating these vulnerable spaces.

Oktapbang 옥탑방 **(Rooftop Room)**

▌**Stranger** 비밀의 숲 2017 • drama

*Often shown as romantic hideouts, rooftop rooms are
actually sweltering in summer and freezing in winter.
In Stranger, Han Yeo-jin (Bae Doo-na) lives here, reflecting
her sense of isolation from the world.*

Goshiwon 고시원
(Tiny Studio Lodging)

▌*Itaewon* **Class**
이태원 클라쓰 2020 • drama

▌**Strangers from Hell**
타인은 지옥이다 2020 • drama

*Cramped rooms for exam-takers
or anyone on a budget. In Itaewon
Class, Park Sae-ro-yi (Park Seo-
joon) plans his comeback in one; in
Strangers from Hell, Jong-woo (Im Si-
wan) moves into a goshiwon filled with
sinister neighbors - changing his life
in ways he never imagined.*

3 The **Korean Chronicles:**
Dramas & Films Through Time

Sometimes, the stories we love are rooted in histories we barely know. Let's take a brief detour into the past - less as memory, more as imagination.

Looking back often evokes nostalgia. But stories set in a past we never lived - untouched by personal memory - stir something else. They invite us into imagined histories, collective longings, and felt realities that seem strangely familiar. Perhaps that's why so many Korean period dramas use time travel - connecting past and present to make both feel alive.

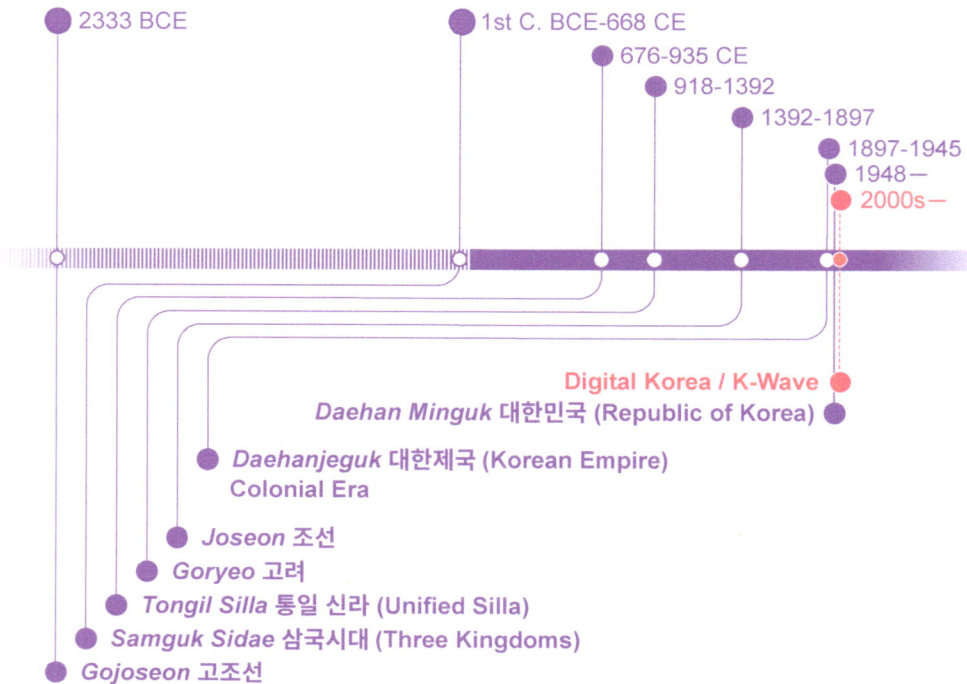

2333 BCE

1st C. BCE-668 CE

676-935 CE

918-1392

1392-1897

1897-1945

1948—

2000s—

Digital Korea / K-Wave

Daehan Minguk 대한민국 (Republic of Korea)

Daehanjeguk 대한제국 (Korean Empire)
Colonial Era

Joseon 조선

Goryeo 고려

Tongil Silla 통일 신라 (Unified Silla)

Samguk Sidae 삼국시대 (Three Kingdoms)

Gojoseon 고조선

NOTE: All dates in this book are given in the Common Era(CE) unless otherwise noted.

In this chapter, we trace the timeline of Korean dramas and films - how they've evolved from royal courts and war-torn lands to high schools, hospitals, and dystopias. As Korea changed, so did its screen stories. Together, they show us not only how far Korea has come but how deeply it continues to resonate.

History class? Too heavy.

*But binge-watching **sageuk** 사극 (historical drama)?*
I'm in - especially if the royal palace is under zombie attack!

One more episode!

Era: *Gojoseon* 고조선 & Three Kingdoms (2333 BCE–668 CE)

Western Parallel: **Greece's Mycenaean palaces to the Roman Empire**

Korea's earliest kingdom begins with a legend: Dangun 단군, the mythical grandson of the heavenly king, born to a bear-turned-woman. While Dangun himself belongs to mythology, the kingdom he is said to have founded - Gojoseon - is considered by many to be the first historical state on the Korean Peninsula. According to the Samguk Yusa 삼국유사, a 13th-century historical text, Gojoseon was founded in 2333 BCE, marking the symbolic beginning of Korean civilization.

During this era, Bronze culture was gradually giving way to iron, and fierce rivalries emerged among tribal unions south of the Han River. These alliances would later evolve into the Three Kingdoms: Goguryeo 고구려, Baekje 백제, and Silla 신라.

During the Three Kingdoms period, Buddhism began to spread across the land, laying cultural and spiritual foundations that would shape Korean identity for centuries to come.

▌Jumong 주몽 2006 • drama

A sweeping saga of the abandoned prince who rises to found Goguryeo. Both heroism and love shape his journey, and his legendary archery still echoes today - as Korean archers continue to dominate the Olympic stage.

Tongil Silla 통일 신라 (Unified Silla) (676 – 935 CE)

Western Parallel: **Early Middle Ages**

The first unified kingdom on the Korean Peninsula, Unified Silla marked a cultural golden age. During this time, Buddhism flourished, influencing everything from temples and sculptures to everyday life. Arts and sciences thrived under royal patronage, with Silla's cultural legacy still influencing Korea today. Among its treasures, the ornate golden crowns of Silla speak volumes - where the "weight of the crown" was both literal and symbolic. Their design isn't just majestic - it's meticulous. Each fine cut and delicate inlay points to a culture that valued beauty, precision, and meaning in every detail.

Queen *Seondeok* 선덕여왕
2009 • drama

The tale of Korea's first female ruler - her rise from princess to monarch, and her struggle for wisdom and power in a male-dominated world.

Era:
Goryeo 고려 Dynasty (918 – 1392 CE)

Western Parallel: **High Middle Ages**

Goryeo was a dynasty of elegance and resilience - surviving invasions, cultivating beauty, and shaping Korea's cultural foundations.

Celadon reached new artistic heights, and printing technology advanced at a pace that stunned the world - Korea's metal movable type predates Gutenberg by nearly two centuries. Civil service exams took root, shaping a merit-based system that echoed for generations.

While Confucianism gained ground, Buddhist temples continued to define the Korean landscape.

▍Korea - Khitan War 고려 거란 전쟁 2023-2024 • drama

The drama portrays a young king of Goryeo who, despite fierce opposition, joins forces with a seasoned general to defend the kingdom against the invading Khitan Empire. It underscores the courage and steadfast loyalty of the commanders who risked everything to safeguard their nation.

Era:
Joseon 조선 Dynasty (1392 – 1897)

Western Parallel: **From the Renaissance to the Rise of Western Empires**

Neo-Confucianism, or seongnihak 성리학, once ruled everyday life, and its influence still echoes through Korean values today. Hangeul 한글 was born, boosting literacy and opening space for storytelling beyond the elite. Class lines were strictly drawn - but slowly bent under the weight of time, money, and survival.

More than anything, Joseon was obsessed with records.

Not just what happened, but how it happened - every deliberation, disagreement, and decision was faithfully recorded, often in real time.

Even the king himself was barred from reading what was written about him.

That obsession with truth and detail lives on - in the richly layered worlds of Korea's historical dramas.

Susu's Box

The Annals of the *Joseon* Dynasty

The Annals of the Joseon Dynasty are an exhaustive record of the reigns of Korea's Joseon kings, spanning roughly 500 years and 25 monarchs.

Dedicated yet stubborn historians, called **sagwan** 사관, documented everything – and anything – related to the kings. One famous episode tells of King Taejo 태조, the founder of Joseon, who once fell off his horse. Embarrassed, he ordered that the incident not be recorded. Thanks to the historians' unwavering commitment to truth, today we even know that the king tried to have it erased. At this point, the royal historians weren't just observers. They were the eyes and the shadows – always watching, always writing.

Preserving the Annals, multiple copies of the Annals were stored in special archives called **sago** 사고, located across different regions to ensure their preservation. Every three years, the stored volumes were brought out and aired under the sun to prevent damage.

Thanks to such unwavering practices, the Annals survived for centuries and remain one of the world's most detailed and reliable royal chronicles – and a treasure trove for Korean historical dramas.

The Throne 사도 2015 • movie

Based on one of the most tragic episodes in Joseon history, The Throne explores the strained relationship between King Yeongjo 영조 and his son, Crown Prince Sado 사도.

As political pressures mount, the crown prince - perceived as unstable and unfit to rule - is locked in a wooden rice chest on royal orders.

Song Kang-ho and Yoo Ah-in are unforgettable in their roles.

The Tale of Lady *Ok* 옥씨 부인전 2024-2025 • drama

The story follows Gudeok - a woman born into slavery who assumes the identity of a noblewoman after a tragic incident.
Played by Im Ji-yeon (The Glory), Gudeok 구덕 reinvents herself as a legal advocate in Joseon's court system, taking the side of the powerless.

Era :
Modern Transition (1897 – 1945)

Western Parallel: **Late Imperialism & World Wars**

Daehanjaeguk, 대한제국(The Korean Empire) had a short and fragile run. But Japan's growing imperial ambitions soon led to Korea's annexation in 1910, beginning 35 years of colonial rule. This was a time of contradiction. Railways were built and modern schools were opened - but always under watch. Resistance took many forms: armed uprisings, underground publications, and a global independence movement.

In this in-between era, modern Korea was born - under occupation, but never in submission.

Chicago Typewriter 시카고 타자기 2017 • drama

A time-slip mystery connecting 1930s colonial Korea with the present, the drama stars Yoo Ah-in as a bestselling author whose life becomes entangled with a ghostwriter - literally a ghost - and a woman, each haunted by memories of a shared past.

Era :
Contemporary Korea I (Korean war to 1988)

Western Parallel: **The Cold War Era, from Containment to Consumerism**

After the Korean War broke out in 1950, the country was torn in two - then slowly rebuilt from ruins. Military regimes seized power, while waves of civil resistance continued to rise.

The Gwangju Uprising (Gwangju Minjuhwa Undong, 광주민주화운동) of 1980 - later depicted in "Human Acts" by Han Kang, who became Korea's first Nobel laureate in 2024 - left a scar that still lingers. Steadfast support came from those who had little, but gave anyway.

Rapid growth followed - but not without hardship. The 1988 Olympics marked Korea's re-entry onto the global stage, carrying the shadows of sacrifice that made it shine.

▌A Taxi Driver 택시 운전사 2017 • movie

Based on a true story, the movie follows Man-seob (Song Kang-ho), a Seoul cabbie just trying to earn a long-distance fare, until a German reporter hires him for a one-day trip to Gwangju. What he thought was a simple ride plunges him into one of Korea's darkest - and bravest - chapters. A story of truth glimpsed through a windshield - and courage found on the run.

Contemporary Korea II (1988 – Now)

Western Parallel: **Globalization & the Digital Age (1980s–Present)**

Democracy strengthened - but not without creative experiments. Like making kimchi pancakes in a waffle maker, Koreans tested many shapes of democracy. Of the six elected presidents in the 21st century, three faced impeachment - and two were actually removed.

Meanwhile, K-Pop rose, followed by the global waves of K-dramas and Webtoons.

Seoul became a 24-hour city - constantly trending, endlessly awake. A place of speed, sparkle, and screens - yet also a city where silence is rare, and rest can make you restless. Digital life replaced everything from cash to conversations on KakaoTalk (카카오톡, Korea's go-to messaging app; often shortened to Katok 카톡). Still, some dream of a world of unplugged, of analog.

▌Unknown Seoul 미지의 서울 2025 • drama

Twin sisters - identical in face but worlds apart in life - decide to switch places, one hoping to ease the burdens of the other. What begins as a small lie soon becomes a journey through love, hardship, and self-discovery. Even their names - Miji 미지 (un-known), and Mirae 미래 (future) - hint at the paths they are about to walk. Tackling themes like workplace bullying, disability, and emotional isolation, this quietly powerful series blends a narrative that carries both weight and warmth.

Susu's Box ....

Dystopian Futures, Korean Style

Rain-slicked streets. Flickering neon. Ominous music. Why is the future always so dark?
From K-dramas to films, Korean creators are imagining worlds shaped not by flying cars - but by anxiety, algorithms, and surveillance. Let's take a look at a story projecting today's fears onto tomorrow's screens.

▌Hellbound 지옥 2021, 2024 • drama

Directed by Yeon Sang-ho (Train to Busan), this chilling series imagines a world where death sentences arrive with exact dates and smoke-born monsters come to claim their due. But the real terror begins after - when fear hardens into faith, and a new order rises from chaos.

▌Duty After School
방과후 전쟁활동 2023 • drama

One day, the sky fills with floating alien orbs. Then comes the government's order: high school seniors will be armed - and deployed. In a country where exams decide everything, students are promised bonus points for serving. What happens when youth is interrupted - not by growing up, but by alien war?

K-Drama Clichés (Quick List)
the tricks you already know by heart.

- **Birth Secret** — hidden parentage / switched-at-birth twist
- **Traffic Grab** (aka Wrist Grab) — pulled from the road; instant closeness
- **Enemies-to-Lovers** — enemies at first, lovers in the end
- **Second-Lead Love Triangle** — aka Second-Lead Syndrome
- **One Heroine, Many Suitors** — everyone falls for the same woman
- **Selective Amnesia** — minor crash, major memory loss
- **Someone Is Always Listening** — the secret gets overheard

I'm not your father.

4 K-Contents Destinations

Sure, some K-dramas take you abroad - Paris, Berlin, Macau, even supposedly Pyongyang (we're looking at you, 'Crash Landing on You'). But most stories unfold right here, across the alleys, rooftops, cafés, and tiny sea-side towns of Korea.

Let's trace the locations - not just where stories were told, but where they were made, lived, and remembered.

Seoul 서울

Rooftops, Rivers, and Endless Scenes

From rooftop chases to riverside dates, Seoul plays it all. 'Itaewon Class', 'Parasite', 'The Glory' - and pretty much every K-drama ever - has passed through its cafés, bridges, and back alleys.

Bonus? Many of these spots are still standing - and surprisingly walkable. You could follow your favorite scenes with just a map and a good pair of shoes.

Top 7 Seoul Spots from K-Pop Demon Hunters

1 *Jamsil* Olympic Stadium (잠실종합경기장)

The very concert hall where Huntrix makes a dramatic drop while performing *How It's Done* in the opening scene.

2 *Lotte* World Tower (롯데월드타워)

Huntrix's penthouse is implied to be here, though the actual tower couldn't appear on-screen due to copyright issues.

3 *Samseong* Station Billboard (삼성역 전광판)

Famous for its hyper-realistic 3D wave video art, this massive screen at Samseong Subway Station makes a cameo in the series.

4 *Bukchon Hanok* Village (북촌한옥마을)

The narrow alley where Lumi and Jinwoo meet after receiving a note from Derpy the Tiger.

5 *Naksan* Park (낙산공원)

Along the fortress wall, this becomes the setting for an action-filled "date" with an enemy.

6 *Namsan* N Tower (남산 N타워)

Initially just part of the background, it transforms into the virtual venue for the Lion Boys' final concert in the climactic scene.

7 *Cheongdam* Bridge (청담대교)

Beneath this span over the Han River, where Seoul Subway Line 7 rumbles past, a high-stakes battle with the demons erupts.

▌Castaway on the Moon 김씨 표류기 | 2009 • movie

A man fails a suicide attempt - and ends up stranded on a tiny, uninhabited island... right in the middle of Seoul's Han River.
Cut off from the world yet surrounded by it, he begins to rediscover life in complete isolation.
Across the river, a reclusive young woman - watching him through a camera lens - forms a silent connection.
It's a story about loneliness, resilience, and longing, with one very specific craving tying them together: a bowl of black bean noodles, jjajangmyeon 짜장면.

The delivery guy arrives - but rescue never does.
A quiet, quirky film that turns the heart of Seoul into a strange kind of wilderness - where two invisible people finally begin to be seen.

▌Itaewon Class 이태원 클라쓰 2020 • drama

*Set in one of Seoul's most eclectic neighborhoods, Itaewon Class is a webtoon-based drama that sparked a cultural wave across Korea and beyond. It follows a group of young dreamers - led by the subtly defiant Park Sae-ro-yi - as they launch a small pub called **Danbam** 단밤, challenging powerful rivals and societal norms along the way.*
More than a story of love and ambition, this series captures the spirit of modern Seoul: its racial diversity, youth culture, and ever-evolving food scene. Filmed near the actual Itaewon subway station - known for brunch spots, nightlife, and open views of Namsan Tower - the show doubles as a visual tour of Seoul's nightscape and indie backstreets.
A must-watch for anyone curious about the bold, rebellious heart of the city.

Gyeonggi Province 경기도

Close to Seoul, Open to Dream

Close to Seoul - but with just enough room to breathe. Suwon gave us the nostalgic glow of 'Our Beloved Summer,' while Yongin Minsokchon 용인 민속촌, (Korean Folk Village) and Paju 파주 (near the DMZ) often play the role of "anywhere in Korea."

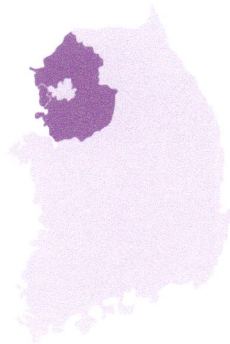

Historic sites, outdoor film sets, and the occasional palace appear more often than you'd expect - sometimes standing in for the past, sometimes just as a perfect backdrop for an intimate conversation.

Suwon 수원

▌Our Beloved Summer 그해 우리는 2021 • drama

Nostalgic, tender, and emotional - Our Beloved Summer unfolds along Suwon's sunlit streets and schoolyards.
He was the once-failing boy who loved to draw (Choi Woo-sik).
She was the top-of-her-class girl who always had a plan (Kim Da-mi).
In high school, they were paired - awkwardly - for a documentary.
Years later, the camera rolls again, and a gentle love story picks up where it left off, winding through the stone walls and leafy paths of Suwon's Hwaseong Fortress.

Filmed in

Hwaseong 화성 & Dongtan 동탄

▌Lovely Runner 선재업고튀어 2024 • drama

Im Sol, given one chance to turn back time, runs to save her star Ryu Seon-jae.
Set among Suwon and Hwaseong's parks, schools, and peaceful streets, the series turns ordinary corners into soft-focus memories of first love, second chances, and sprinting toward what matters most.

Gangwon Province 강원도

Foggy Skies, Lonely Goodbyes

Need emotional impact? Cue Gangwon 강원. Dramas love its foggy coastlines, windy beaches, and the kind of train stations that seem built for eternal goodbyes. It's where lovers part in silence, and where characters walk alone - just before or after a life-altering event. From quiet fishing villages and rugged shores to deep mountain trails, Gangwon offers that rare cinematic combination: stillness and tension in the same frame.

Crash Landing on You 사랑의 불시착 2019 • drama

A modern-day Romeo and Juliet, set against the backdrop of a divided Korea.
When Yoon Se-ri - an elegant, sharp-tongued heiress - crash-lands in North Korea during a paragliding accident, she's rescued by stoic officer Ri Jeong-hyeok.
Beyond survival, she finds warmth, loyalty, and an unexpected love that gradually transforms her; in real life, their on-screen love blossomed into marriage.

Filming Note : Though the story begins in North Korea, the iconic paragliding scene was filmed at Byeolmaro Observatory (별마로 천문대) in Yeongwol 영월, Gangwon Province.

One Fine Spring Day 봄날은 간다 2001 • movie

Set in Gangwon's quiet countryside and misty coast, the film follows a sound engineer - who records the wind in bamboo forests - and a radio producer. Like the season it's named after, their romance fades softly, almost unnoticed.
Lines like "How can love change?" and "Do you want some ramyeon?" - the original "Netflix and chill?" - still echo today.

Chungcheong Area 충청지역

Quiet Fields, Built for Stories

Need stillness and sincerity? Chungcheong 충청 has both - and more. From peaceful rural landscapes to wide-open university campuses perfect for slow walks and reflective scenes, the region offers cinematic calm at every turn. With Daejeon 대전 at its center, crews benefit from easy nationwide access and a growing network of modern production studios capable of hosting even large-scale shoots.

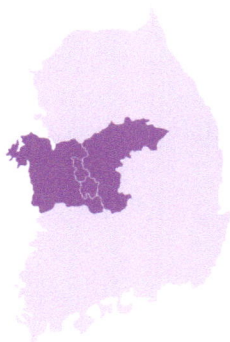

Across the plains, hills, and cities of Chungcheong, filmmakers have found places that seem to pause time - ideal for stories set in the past, the present, or somewhere in between.

Location
Dajeon 대전 — University Campuses & Filming Studios

Boyhood 소년시대 2023 • drama

Set in 1989, in the rural towns of South Chungcheong Province - though filmed mostly in Gyeonggi and Gangwon. Byung-tae (Im Si-wan) is a timid teen whose only wish is to survive school unscathed.
But when he's mistaken for a legendary fighter of the same name, he's pulled into the brutal, hierarchy-obsessed world of schoolyard politics.

CNU White Horse Statue
— where Im Sol wakes after her time slip in 'Lovely Runner.'

Located in the heart of South Korea, Daejeon's central access and diverse landscapes have made it a popular backdrop for film and television. Its university campuses and local studios have hosted a wide range of productions - from campus scenes to dark, dystopian thrillers.

Films and dramas like 'No Breathing,' 'Dr. Romantic 2,' 'True Beauty,' 'Doona!,' and 'A Killer Paradox' shot key lecture hall scenes at Daejeon University - while 'Lovely Runner' was filmed at nearby Chungnam National University (CNU). Even Netflix hits like Squid Game and Hellbound were filmed at Daejeon-based studios, solidifying the city's reputation as a rising production hub.

One behind-the-scenes tidbit: a performer whose hands appeared as a double in 'Squid Game''s gonggi 공기 scene visited the Daejeon studio - and later shared a story about meeting several of the show's stars.

Jeonju 전주 & Jeolla Area 전라지역

Tiled Roofs, Timeless Flavors

Jeonju's hanok village 전주 한옥 마을 is basically a film set already. Whether it's period dramas or modern retellings, the contrast between curved tiled roofs and stylish cafés is always camera-ready. 'Mr. Sunshine' and countless *sageuk* 사극 (historical dramas) owe much to Jeonju's preserved charm.

But Jeolla 전라 isn't just known for atmosphere - it's Korea's culinary capital. And in a recent drama, actress Go Min-si brought it full circle, playing a chef based in Jeonju.

▌Your Taste 당신의 맛 2025 • drama

This drama follows a rising chef who returns to her hometown - famous for its culinary pride - to rediscover flavors, memories, and herself. As her rustic charm clashes with a recipe-hunting chaebol heir, their awkward yet endearing connection slowly simmers into something more.
Set mostly in Jeonju hanok village, the drama unfolds at a gentle pace with limited sets. The storytelling is loose, the direction unhurried—sometimes uneven, but oddly fitting.

▌The Wailing 곡성 2016 • movie

Set in the misty mountains of Gokseong 곡성 - a real village in Korea, where the film was also shot, this masterfully crafted thriller begins with brutal murders and a strange illness that unsettles a quiet rural community.
Visually haunting and narratively gripping, The Wailing leaves viewers disturbed, fascinated, and haunted long after the final scene.

Busan 부산 & Gyeongsang Area 경상지역

Oceans, Hills and Raw Edges

Busan 부산 gives edge. From Park Chan-wook's 'Decision to Leave' to countless noir-ish thrillers, its steep hills and hazy harbor views have become cinematic staples.

But it's more than sea, romance, and crime. As the final stop on Korea's main railway line - and once a wartime refuge during the Korean War - it's also where desperate passengers ran from zombies in 'Train to Busan'.

A little raw, a little cinematic - Busan doesn't just set the scene. It sharpens it.

▌Pachinko 파친코 2022- • drama

Spanning generations, wars, and oceans, Pachinko follows a Korean family whose lives unfold across Busan, Osaka, and New York.
At its heart is Sunja (Kim Min-ha), whose quiet strength shapes a legacy of love, loss, and migration.
From the markets of colonial-era Korea to the neon-lit alleys of postwar Japan, the drama traces history's rhythms through the people who lived them.

▌Train to *Busan* 부산행 2016 • movie

A viral outbreak - sparked, some say, by a gorani 고라니, (see Creatures of K) - plunges South Korea into chaos, turning one train into a desperate escape route. As the KTX speeds toward Busan, passengers must fight not only to survive, but to protect each other.
At the heart is a father, realizing too late what it means to live for someone else.
More than a zombie thriller, Train to Busan is a story of sacrifice, urgency, and the fragile ties that hold us together when the world comes apart.

Jeju Island 제주도

Winds, Wonders, and Slow Escapes

They say Jeju 제주 isn't just a place - it's a state of mind, a way of life.

This southern island, shaped by fire and wind, has become Korea's ultimate escape. Once known mostly as a honeymoon destination, Jeju is now a favorite among creators and artists.

Volcanic cliffs, stone-walled roads, misty forests, and the slow pace of island life make it feel like another world entirely - yet it's just an hour's flight from Seoul.

Our Blues 우리들의 블루스 2022 • drama

Set entirely on Jeju Island, Our Blues weaves together the layered lives of ordinary people - vendors, divers, young lovers, estranged mothers and daughters - each revealing different shades of love, regret, and resilience. Against the backdrop of Jeju's coastline, traditional markets, and winding stone-walled villages, their stories unfold in quiet, loosely connected episodes that feel both personal and universal.
Our Blues is a love letter to life's fragile, yet softly radiant moments.

K-Pop Demon Hunters
– *Seonangdang* 서낭당

A sacred site in Korea's indigenous folk religion, dedicated to the Seonang spirit believed to protect the village. it appears in Lumi's childhood flashback and in a later episode with Celine.

– in Jeju Folk Village –

▌When Life Gives You Tangerines

폭싹 속았수다 2024 • drama

Begun in the stone-walled villages of Jeju, the drama traces the lifelong journey of Ae-soon and Gwan-sik - two islanders born under a heavy sky but carrying a quiet, stubborn light in their hearts.
Anchored by the performances of three generations of actors, and supported by a rich cast, this is a story woven with unforgettable lines and lived-in moments - lingering like salt in sea air. Jeju's iconic locations serve as both backdrop and character: from Seongsan Ilchulbong 성산 일출봉 rising over canola fields where Ae-soon makes her 3,000 bows, to Seogwipo Maeil Olle Market 서귀포 매일 올레 시장 where Gwan-sik stands guard at her cabbage stall.

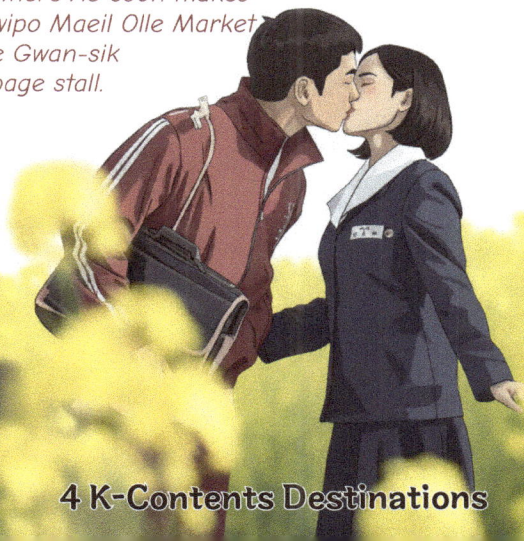

▌Welcome to *Samdal-ri* 웰컴투 삼달리 2023-2024 • drama

When a high-flying fashion photographer (Shin Hae-seon) hits rock bottom, she escapes to the one place she thought she'd left behind forever - her seaside hometown, Samdal-ri 삼달리. There, childhood memories and long-lost love stir back to life - especially in the form of a steadfast weatherman (Ji Chang-wook) who never quite moved on. Set on Jeju Island, the drama paints the island not as a tourist escape, but as a lived-in place - full of wind and stubborn hearts. More than a romance, it's a story of return: of identity reclaimed, and love rediscovered in the place that raised you.

Susu's Box

Makjang 막장, but Make It Korean

In some Korean dramas, betrayal and lies, secret births, chaebols, murder, misunderstandings, and loyal sidekicks all collide – sometimes within a single episode. People die, only to come back alive.

This is Makjang: a beautiful mess where logic kneels before drama. The story only works if everyone watching silently agrees: "Okay... let's just go with it."

NEW ME!

By the way,

'Makjang' originally means the very end of a mining tunnel — the place where you literally can't go any further.

Famous *Makjang* dramas

▌**The Mermaid** 인어공주 2002
▌*Jang Bo-ri* Is Here! 왔다 장보리 2014
▌**The Penthouse 1,2,3** 펜트하우스 2020-2021

Legendary *Makjang* !!

▌**Temptation of Wife** 아내의 유혹 2008

A betrayed wife returns from the dead (well, kind of) for the ultimate revenge. With one well-placed beauty mark and a sharp new eyeliner, no one recognizes her - perfect disguise, perfect payback. The drama that launched a thousand memes, Temptation of Wife is outrageous, iconic, and impossible to forget.

The World of K-Webtoons — Going Vertical, Going Digital

Webtoons? Yep, they aren't just doodles - they're the lifeblood of K-dramas, a stream of stories that never stops. Not your average comics. Born in the early 2000s in Korea, these vertical, full-color scrolls were designed for screens, not pages - for subway rides and bus stops, not bookstores.

With no gutters to interrupt the flow, webtoons feel more like film than print: a frame-by-frame immersion with cinematic pacing and emotional punch. Once considered niche, webtoons have evolved into a flexible format - hosting everything from fantasy to memoir, romance to reportage. They're also one of K-drama's richest source materials.

From Korea to the World

Two platforms shaped the wave: Daum Webtoon 다음 웹툰 (now Kakao Page), and Naver Webtoon 네이버 웹툰 (branded WEBTOON globally). In the early days, Daum took the first creative leap - most notably with Kang Full, author of 'Moving' and 'Light House', both adapted into Disney+ Originals (2023 and 2024). He broke the comic mold by treating human stories as serious narrative art.

Naver followed and eventually overtook the scene with breakout titles like 'The Sound of Your Heart' (2006-2020), transformed into both animation and web drama, blending absurdity with serialized momentum. Today, Korean webtoons are translated into dozens of languages and adapted into global hits like 'Itaewon Class', 'All of Us Are Dead', and 'Weak Hero Class 1'.

Webtoons may be sleek, fast, and wildly addictive - but their production is anything but effortless. Behind the digital polish lies a creative grind. Many artists work under brutal schedules - weekly updates, sometimes multiple per week.
And now, as AI enters the webtoon space, new questions are emerging: What is authorship? Can storytelling be automated? If so, to what extent - and should it?

12 Webtoons You've Probably Seen on Screen

1 Cheese in the Trap 치즈 인더 트랩 2016
Awkward, smart, and romantically complicated

2 Sweet Home 스위트 홈 2020-2024
Grief and fear turn into monsters in a collapsing apartment complex. Amid the chaos, neighbors who once lived as strangers must band together to survive.

3 *Misaeng* 미생 2014

A failed baduk (Go) prodigy enters corporate life, where each deal and relationship becomes another move on the board in his struggle for survival.

4 Solo Leveling 나혼자만 레벨업 2025-

A powerless hunter fights through a brutal world where strength defines survival. Based on a hit web novel and webtoon - adapted into anime in Japan, with a live-action drama also in the works.

5 All of Us Are Dead 지금 우리 학교는 2022

A viral outbreak traps students in school, forcing them to fight, change, and choose.

6 Light Shop 조명가게 2024

Lost souls visit a mysterious lamp store, where flickering light reveals the grief they couldn't let go.

7 Business Proposal 사내 맞선 2022

A fake date turns dangerously real when a food product developer discovers her blind date is... her company's CEO. What begins as a comic misunderstanding soon blossoms into office romance, complete with secret meetings and unexpected sparks. Ahn Hyo Seop, the voice actor of Jinwoo from Saja Boys plays the role of the CEO.

8 Reborn Rich 재벌집 막내아들 2022

After betrayal and death, a loyal secretary is reborn as the youngest son of the chaebol family he once served, navigating revenge, power, and fate in a world of wealth.

9 Weak Hero Class1 약한 영웅1 2022

A quiet top student becomes a precise and relentless fighter when school violence pushes him too far.

10 Yumi's Cells 1,2 유미의 세포들 1,2 2021-2022

"Inside Out," but for dating, deadlines, and the dreams we're told to outgrow - Yumi's life is run by tiny, opinionated cells with a lot to say

11 Daily Dose of Sunshine 정신병동에도 아침이 와요 2023

A rookie nurse joins the psychiatric ward, learning that healing flows both ways. Based on the webtoon memoir of a real-life nurse.

12 Bloodhounds of Duty 중증외상센터: 골든 아워 2025

Trauma surgeons race the clock to save lives - the series blends sharp realism with emotionally grounded characters. Amidst the chaos of the ER, it highlights both the fragility of life and the resilience of those who fight to preserve it.

Storyboard Like a Webtoon, Storytell Like a Korean

Bong Joon-ho

Long before the Oscars, Bong Joon-ho 봉준호 was already sketching worlds. A devoted comic book fan, he drew editorial cartoons for his campus paper. Known for his obsessive attention to detail, he would later earn the nickname "Bong-tail" - a nod to his storyboard precision, where every frame feels like a scene from a finished film.

Dir. Hong

Dir. Bong

Unlike Hong Sang-soo 홍상수 who often shoots without a script, capturing spontaneity on set - Bong plans every frame in advance. Two radically different styles, yet both deeply Korean in rhythm and restraint.

As actor Chris Evans once said of filming 'Snowpiercer 2013': "Bong doesn't shoot and then edit. He shoots exactly according to the edit he's already completed in his head - like building a house and saying, 'I need 53 nails,' not 'A sack of nails.'"

In Bong's world, every shot is already locked. No wasted footage. No extra nails.

The Dong-A Ilbo, Interview with Bong Joon-ho (June 11, 2019)

5 Street Food to Soul Food

Koreans love to eat - perhaps even more so than people elsewhere in the world. This passion shows not only in the flavors on the table, but also in how deeply food is woven into everyday language and social life.

When greeting someone, it's common to ask, "Did you eat?" (밥 먹었어?) - a question that goes beyond politeness. Making plans can be as simple as, "Let's have a meal together soon" (밥 한 번 먹자) or even, "Let's grab a coffee" (차 한 번 마시자).

The verb to eat infuses the Korean lexicon, spawning expressions that serve as metaphor, humor, or emotional shorthand:

Korean Expression / English Meaning

to eat one's heart 마음을 먹다
➡ to resolve or make a firm decision, often with emotional weight

to eat age 나이 먹다
➡ to get older, to age (a natural way of saying "grow old")

to peel and eat 까먹다
➡ to forget completely, as if memory were eaten up

to eat a friend 친구 먹다
➡ to become friends

to eat insults 욕 먹다
➡ to be scolded or criticized, to receive harsh words

If you say so

Let's be friends!

There's even a running joke among patients: upon being diagnosed, the first question is often, "What should I eat to cure this?"

And then there's **mukbang** 먹방 - livestreams where slim hosts devour absurd amounts of food while chatting with viewers. For some, watching others eat can be strangely satisfying, almost as if the act of eating has been shared across a screen.

In a country where even emotions are "eaten," food fills not just the bowl, but the heart.

Jipbap 집밥 : the Quiet Strength That Keeps Us Going

In Korea, *jipbap* 집밥 - literally house 집 + rice 밥, or a home-cooked meal - means more than just food. It's warmth. It's someone remembering what you like and gently placing it on your plate.

There's even a word *bapsim* 밥심 - rice + strength - the steady energy that keeps you going.

The word *sikgu* 식구 literally means "meal family" - those who eat together. Even after long silences or hard days, sharing a bowl of soup often says what words can't.

And you'll see it in every drama: a late-night phone call, a cracked voice on the line. The question is rarely "How are you?" but instead - "Did you eat?" (밥은 먹었어?)

Bap 밥 (Rice Dishes)

At the heart of most Korean meals, *bap* 밥 is more than just food - it's what fills you, grounds you, and brings everyone to the table.

Traditionally, bap refers to plain steamed white rice served with **banchan** 반찬 (side dishes). But in Korean culture, the word has expanded to mean "a meal" itself. For example, **achim-bap** 아침밥 doesn't only mean "morning + cooked rice," but also simply "breakfast."

Kimbap 김밥

Seaweed-wrapped rice rolls filled with proteins and vegetables in balanced colors. Korea's ultimate portable meal on the go.

Bibimbap 비빔밥

A bowl of warm rice topped with vegetables, meat, and spicy gochujang - or a milder soy-based sauce.

Kimchi Fried Rice 김치볶음밥

Stir-fried rice with aged kimchi (except cucumber kimchi), often mixed with spam or **samgyeopsal** 삼겹살 (pork belly).

▌**Extraordinary Attorney *Woo*** 이상한 변호사 우영우 2022 • drama

In Extraordinary Attorney Woo, Woo Young-woo (played by Park Eun-bin), an autistic attorney with a brilliant mind, prefers food that is predictable and never surprises her - like kimbap.
Her father even opens a kimbap shop, showing how central the dish is to their lives. Woo Young-woo, a devoted fan of kimbap, once says:

See also: K for Kimbap on Netflix 2025

"Kimbap is trustworthy. The seaweed, rice, carrots, eggs, burdock root, and spinach... they're always in the same place, and no ingredient invades another's space. That's why kimbap is always predictable and safe to eat."

Kimchi 김치 (Key Ingredient)

Kimchi is more than a side dish - it's a culture fermented into the Korean DNA. Made by salting and seasoning vegetables with garlic, chili flakes, and other spices, kimchi comes in countless varieties. Each family has its own recipe, often passed down like a well-kept secret.

There's an old joke: Ask your Korean friend, "Is it true you have a fridge just for kimchi?" And 100% of the time, you'll hear: "Not every Korean home has one... but we do."

Kimchi isn't just for the side of the plate - it's folded into pancakes, dumplings, stews, and fried rice. And once a year, there's ***Kimjang*** 김장 - the grand, communal event where families make enough kimchi to last the whole winter. Some households make over a hundred heads of cabbage in one go.

Chemistry of Kimchi

Kimchi starts with salting vegetables - this draws out moisture, softens the texture, and creates a salty environment that suppresses harmful bacteria. Garlic, ginger, chili powder, and often fish sauce are then added, along with a starch-based porridge that provides sugars for fermentation. Over time, naturally occurring lactic acid bacteria (LAB) begin to thrive, converting those sugars into lactic acid, lowering the pH and giving kimchi its signature tang. This slow microbial transformation not only preserves the food but deepens its flavor and enhances its probiotic value.

Types of Kimchi

Baechu Kimchi
배추김치

The classic napa cabbage kimchi. Spicy, fermented, and essential - it's the one most people mean when they say "kimchi."

Kkakdugi 깍두기

Diced radish kimchi with a crisp texture and tangy kick. A perfect companion to hot soups like seolleongtang or galbitang.
Its cube-like cut is called **kkakduk-sseolgi** 깍둑썰기 - a method of chopping ingredients into neat little blocks.

Oi Sobagi 오이소배기

Think of it as a cucumber salad - with a spicy, garlicky filling of buchu chives. Refreshing and juicy, this kimchi doesn't wait around.
It's made for summer tables, not long-term jars.

Baek Kimchi 백김치

White kimchi made without chili flakes. Mild, clean, and refreshing - like a Korean cousin to pickled vegetables.

Jjigae 찌개 & *Guk* 국 (Stews & Soups)

If rice is the backbone of a Korean meal, *jjigae* 찌개 is its warm, beating heart. Rich, hearty, and full of bold flavor, Korean stews are typically served bubbling hot at the center of the table - meant to be shared, family-style.

They're made with everything from fermented soybean paste and kimchi to anchovies, *dubu* 두부 (tofu), and slices of meat - each recipe offering its own personality of spice and comfort.

Popular Jjigae & Guk

Doenjang Jjigae 된장찌개

A savory stew made with fermented *doenjang* 된장 (soybean paste), dubu, vegetables, and sometimes meat. Deep and earthy, it's a staple in many Korean households.

Kimchi Jjigae 김치찌개

A tangy, spicy stew with aged kimchi, dubu, and often pork or tuna. It's one of the most beloved jjigae varieties - perfect for using up old kimchi and warming both stomach and soul.

Sundubu Jjigae 순두부찌개

A soft tofu stew made with *sundubu* 순두부 (uncurdled dubu), vegetables, and sometimes seafood, in a spicy or milky-white broth. Silky and bubbling, it's a go-to comfort food on chilly days.

Miyeok Guk 미역국

A light, nutritious soup made with *miyeok* 미역 (seaweed), simmered with beef or seafood. Traditionally served on birthdays and after childbirth. And yes - so iconic that there's even a backhanded insult: **"Did your mom even eat miyeok guk after giving birth to you?"** Translation: You weren't even worth a bowl of soup.

Note ： Thick *jjigae* 찌개, balanced *guk* 국, and clear *tang* 탕 - Korean soups vary by how rich the broth is.

Spam & Budae-jjigae:
A Stew Born from Hard Times

Spam arrived in Korea not just as food, but as a lifeline. In the years after the Korean War, when supplies were scarce, U.S. army bases in towns like Uijeongbu 의정부 and Dongducheon 동두천 handed out - or leaked out - surplus rations. Locals mixed those unfamiliar pink slices with kimchi and a spoonful of gochujang, creating a pot of something warming, filling, and new. That was the beginning of *budae-jjigae* 부대찌개, literally "army base stew."

Over time, the recipe shifted from survival to comfort. Spam, sausages, tofu, and vegetables became regular ingredients, with a packet of ramen noodles often dropped in for good measure. Today, budae-jjigae is less about making do and more about gathering around a bubbling pot.

Korea, now the second-largest consumer of Spam after the U.S., even exchanges Spam gift sets during Chuseok, Korean Thanksgiving, and Lunar New Year. From post-war hardship to holiday tradition, Spam has found an unlikely but lasting home in Korean kitchens.

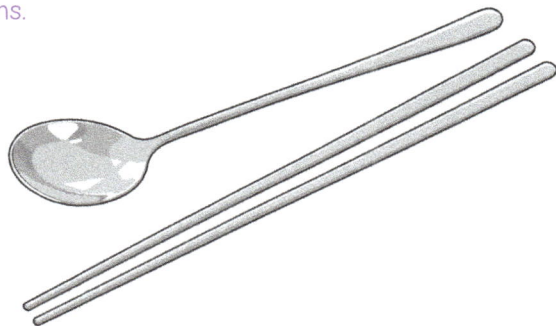

What's for **Lunch** at **School?**

In Korean elementary, middle, and high schools, lunch is carefully planned by professional nutritionists. Schools are encouraged to use sustainable ingredients and locally sourced produce. Most schools have their own kitchens, so meals are freshly prepared on site.

But school lunch is more than just food - it's also an important part of community life, where students gather and share a meal together. While the menu is usually based on traditional Korean cuisine, these days schools often include dishes from other cultures, as well as special themed meals and event menus.

So, what does a typical Korean school lunch tray look like? Let's take a closer look!

Entrées (Meat & Hearty Dishes)

Korean main dishes often center around meat - grilled, braised, stewed, or stuffed. They're typically served with rice and a colorful spread of **banchan** 반찬 (side dishes). Whether sizzling on a tabletop grill or simmering in a pot for hours, these meals fill your belly - and stay with you long after the last bite.

Signature Entrées

Samgyeopsal 삼겹살

Thick slices of pork belly, grilled right at the table, then wrapped in lettuce with **ssamjang** 쌈장, a thick, salty-and-spicy paste, garlic, and fresh vegetables. It's more than just a dish - it's a ritual. For many Korean office workers, gathering on a Friday night over sizzling samgyeopsal and glasses of **soju** 소주 (a distilled Korean liquor) is the ultimate way to close the week.

See also: Samgyeopsal Rhapsody on Netflix 2020

Bulgogi 불고기

Thinly sliced beef marinated in soy, garlic, and sesame oil - sweet-savory, versatile, and always a crowd favorite. Often enjoyed with rice, or as a sweet-and-savory match with **naengmyeon** 냉면 (cold noodles).

Seolleongtang 설렁탕

A slow-simmered ox bone soup, cloudy-white and deeply comforting, paired with rice and kimchi.

Samgyetang 삼계탕

A whole chicken stuffed with rice and ginseng, eaten on Korea's hottest days as a ritual of "fighting heat with heat."

Chimaek 치맥:

Fried Chicken & Beer, Korean-Style

This crispy fried chicken -originally inspired by Southern-style cooking - has surprisingly become one of Korea's national dishes. Paired with beer, *chimaek* 치맥 (chicken 치킨 + *maekju* 맥주 (beer)) isn't just a combo - it's a ritual. A mood. A moment.

When the Korean team plays in the World Cup, chicken joints start gearing up the night before - because they know what's coming. At the Han River park, you can have it delivered straight to your picnic mat.

Korea is home to countless fried chicken chains and flavors - from honey garlic to twoomba, a creamy, spicy sauce with cult status. And no matter the flavor, one thing always comes on the side: cold, crunchy *chikin-mu* 치킨무 (pickled radish).

See also: Chicken Rhapsody on Netflix 2024

Myeon 면 Noodles

Aside from *naengmyeon* 냉면, which is made with buckwheat, most Korean noodles are wheat-based - humble, comforting dishes that fill the in-between moments of daily life. There are two main types: noodles served in hot or cold broth, and noodles mixed with sauce.

From *kalguksu* 칼국수 (knife-cut noodles in broth) to *ramyeon* 라면, these are budget-friendly, belly-warming meals that have fueled generations.

And in modern Korea, ramyeon(not ramen in Japanese style) - whether made from a packet or prepared in a cup - is more than food. It's a pantry staple, a midnight ritual, a cultural constant.

After a fierce internal competition (and a few slurping tests), here are the three noodle champions that made the final cut.

Types of Noodle

Ramyeon 라면

In Korea, ramyeon usually means instant noodles - in a bag or a cup, spicy or soupy, always dependable. The love for ramyeon could fill an entire book... so we'll leave that to Susucat.

Naengmyeon 냉면

Cold buckwheat noodles served in icy broth - or sometimes tossed in spicy sauce. Originally from North Korea, naengmyeon comes with slices of beef, pickled radish, and half a hard-boiled egg. There are several regional styles, but *Pyeongyang naengmyeon* 평양냉면 stands out as the most deceptively challenging - subtle, savory, and surprisingly polarizing.

Jjajangmyeon 짜장면

Wheat noodles topped with rich black bean sauce, diced pork, and vegetables.
It's Korea's ultimate delivery food - and the classic moving day meal, all in one bite.

See also:
Jjajangmyeon Rhapsody on Netflix 2024

Susu's Box

Ramyeon Battle & the New Rising Star

The battle of flavors continues - with Shin Ramyeon's 신라면 fiery broth, bibim-myeon's 비빔면 cold, spicy kick, and Jjapagetti's 짜파게티 (a mash-up of *jjajangmyeon* 짜장면 and spaghetti) rich black bean sauce: the holy trinity of Korean instant noodles.

But the real star of the show? Buldak Bokkeummyeon 불닭볶음면 - blazingly hot, weirdly addictive, and now a genre of its own.

These four legends have become more than noodles. They've become cravings, comfort, and cultural shorthand. And let's not forget the humble cup ramyeon from convenience stores. Eaten late at night while sitting outside a convenience store, it's not just food—it's a rite of passage.

Susu's favorite? Buldak Bokkeummyeon, of course - best with finely shredded cabbage and a scoop of sweetcorn on the side.

Oh, and did you know? At one point, the Danish government labeled Buldak a national health risk and pulled it from shelves. When they reversed the ban, Danes literally celebrated on a boat, dancing with Hochi 호치 (yes, the Buldak mascot), and shouting:

"Freedom for the spice!"

A nation of
Ramyeon Lovers

Koreans eat an average of 77 servings of instant noodles per person every year (World Instant Noodles Association, 2023) - the second highest in the world, after Vietnam. That love story began in 1963, when Samyang 삼양 launched Korea's first ramyeon - born out of postwar scarcity, but soon embraced as comfort food.

By the 1980s, Nongshim 농심 surged ahead with hit after hit: Neoguri 너구리 (thick noodles with seaweed), Yukgaejang Bowl Noodles 육개장면 (thin noodles with spicy broth), Ansungtangmyun 안성탕면 (the "standard"), Jjapaghetti 짜파게티 (black bean noodles reimagined), and of course Shin Ramyeon 신라면 - the catalyst of Korea's enduring love for spice.

For decades, Samyang lagged behind. But in the 2020s, its Buldak Bokkeummyeon 불닭볶음면 made a fiery comeback - spreading worldwide through social media and creating a devoted cult following. (Fun fact: the project was spearheaded by the founder's daughter-in-law - not very common in Korea.)

Another household staple is Ottogi's Jin Ramyeon 오뚜기 진라면 - often called the nation's everyday noodle. Affordable, mild or spicy, it has long been the go-to choice for dorms, army bases, and family kitchens alike. In Korea, the spicy flavor dominates - leaving the mild version often untouched on shelves. In Japan, the opposite holds true: mild sells out faster, while spicy flavors linger.

And in one hit global animation, the Huntrix members are shown eating cup ramyeon that must be left for exactly three minutes before the lid is peeled back - a detail that fans say feels closest to Jin Ramyeon.

Finally, another key player, Paldo 팔도, introduced Bibimmyeon 비빔면 - the original cold, sauce-mixed noodle - and later Wang Ttukgeong 왕뚜껑 (a jumbo bowl noodle). It also found unexpected fame abroad with Dosirak noodles 도시락면 ("lunch box" noodles). In Russia, it became so popular that Доширак (Doh-shee-rahk) now refers to cup ramyeon in general.

Ramyeon, too, is a battlefield - where Korea's love of food meets its unavoidable competitiveness.

Tteok 떡 Rice Cakes

Tteok, or Korean rice cakes, have long held a special place in Korean cuisine - both as festive treats and everyday comfort food. Sweet, colorful versions are enjoyed as snacks, while plain white rice cakes often serve as a chewy base in heartier dishes.

Their texture can be unfamiliar to some, but tteok is gaining fans around the world - especially thanks to the global love for spicy *tteokbokki* 떡볶이.

Songpyeon 송편

Half-moon rice cakes shared at Chuseok, symbolizing family and harvest.

Tteokguk 떡국

Sliced rice cake soup eaten at Lunar New Year - legend says you gain a year of age with every bowl.

Tteokbokki 떡볶이

Soft rice cakes simmered in gochujang-based spicy sauce with garlic, scallions, and often fish cakes or boiled eggs. A beloved Korean soul food. Once a school snack, now a nationwide obsession.
These days, it comes in all flavors - rose, mala, even cream basil.

후식 & 음료 Traditional Sweets & Drinks

Korean desserts often blur the line between meals and sweets - many are rice- or flour-based and just as filling as a small dish. And when it comes to drinks, Korea offers both creamy rice-based refreshers and fermented rice wines that sit somewhere between tradition and trend.

Makgeolli 막걸리

Cloudy, lightly sparkling rice wine - classic with pancakes on rainy days, now a craft trend too.
It also goes well with *jeon* 전, Korean pancakes.

Sikhye 식혜

Sweet, malty rice drink served cold, with tiny grains floating like confetti.

Yakgwa 약과

Honey-ginger pastry, once a ceremonial sweet, now a café and convenience-store favorite.

Bungeoppang and the Art of Living Well

In Korea, people often describe a good neighborhood by what's nearby. Live near a subway? That's *yeok-se-gwon* 역세권. Near a Starbucks? *Sse-se-gwon* 스세권. But in winter, the real dream is *bung-se-gwon* 붕세권: living close to a *bungeoppang* 붕어빵 (fish-shaped pastry) stand.

Crispy on the outside and filled with sweet red bean paste or custard, bungeoppang is beloved street food. And no - there's no actual fish inside. Just warm, sweet comfort on a cold day.

Food Stories:
Seen, Tasted & Felt

▌Let's Eat 2 식사를 합시다 2 2015 • drama

A slice-of-life drama where neighbors bond over food and unexpected friendships.
Each episode lingers on detailed shots of Korean comfort food - warm, inviting, and grounding everyday life. Starring Yoon Doo-joon and Seo Hyun-jin - former K-Pop idols turned actors - the series charms with its warm relationships and grounded humor.

▌It Might Be a Little Spicy Today
오늘은 좀 매울지도 몰라 2022 • drama

Based on a real-life essay, this gentle drama follows an ex-husband learning to cook for his terminally ill ex-wife and their teenage son. Through everyday dishes - sometimes clumsy, sometimes tender - he rebuilds lost bonds and shared memories.
As the story reminds us, food stirs memories and even softens the hardest ones.

Culinary War 흑백요리사 2024 • show

A high-energy cooking competition where Black Spoon underdogs face White Spoon veterans.
The notorious "tofu mountain" challenge - endless tofu dishes in one round - became the show's fiery symbol of creativity under pressure.

Little Forest 리틀 포레스트 2018 • movie

Burned out in the city, Haewon returns to her rural hometown and her mother's kitchen.
There, among fields and seasons, she cooks the meals she once shared - cabbage pancakes, sujebi, cucumber noodles, kimchi fritters.
Through food, nature, and the people around her, she rediscovers balance and the inner strength to begin again.

Please Take Care of My Refrigerator
냉장고를 부탁해 2014– present • show

What's hiding in a celebrity's fridge? Star chefs pull out surprise ingredients and turn them into instant culinary creations.
Every week, a fresh cook-off unfolds - equal parts entertainment, creativity, and flavor.

Mr. Queen 철인왕후 2020-2021 • drama

A sharp-tongued Blue House chef wakes up in the body of a Joseon queen. Determined to find a way back to the present, he takes command of the royal kitchen - only to spar with a king who seems like a puppet but hides secret plans.
A body-swap rom-com where palace politics meet culinary chaos.

Bon Appétit, Majesty! 폭군의 셰프 2025 • drama

A star French-cuisine champion, Chef Yeon Ji-young, is hurled back in time - straight into the court of a tyrant king with an absolute palate.
Caught between royal politics, diplomatic banquets, and a clash of cultures, she serves dishes that can turn even a tyrant's heart.
A survival romantic comedy where Korean and French fusion cuisine dazzles the eyes as much as it stirs the soul.

The Compact Korean Pantry :

Listed brands represent leading options, easy to find in Korean grocery stores overseas as well as online.

1 *Ganjang* 간장 **(Brewed Soy Sauce)**
For general seasoning, stir-fry, and dressings. Standard soy sauce if only one is used. Room temp 6–12 months after opening. Brand: Sempio, Chungjungone

2 *Guk-ganjang* 국간장 **(Soup Soy Sauce)**
Saltier and lighter in color. Used in soups, stews, and vegetable seasoning. Room temp 6–12 months after opening. Brand: Sempio, Chungjungone

3 *Doenjang* 된장 **(Fermented Soybean Paste)**
Deep, salty flavor for stews, soups, dressings, and sauces. Refrigerate after opening. Brands: Sempio, Haechandle (CJ), Sunchang (Chungjungone)

4 *Gochujang* 고추장 **(Fermented Chili Paste)**
Sweet heat with fermented depth. Essential for bibimbap, spicy stews, and sauces. Refrigerate after opening. Brands: Haechandle (CJ), Sunchang (Chungjungone)

5 *Ssamjang* 쌈장 **(Soybean-Chili Paste Mix)**
Used with vegetable wraps. Often includes garlic, sesame, or nuts. Refrigerate after opening. Brands: Haechandle (CJ), Sunchang (Chungjungone)

6 *Gochugaru* 고춧가루 **(Chili Flakes)**
Coarse or fine flakes used in kimchi and stews. Adds heat, color, and aroma. Wide range from small producers to major brands. Store airtight in a cool, dry place.

7 *Seoltang* 설탕 **(Sugar)**

White or brown sugar. Delivers the "sweet" in Korea's sweet-salty-spicy flavor trifecta. Used in marinades, sauces, and stir-fries.

8 *Myeolchi Aekjeot* 멸치액젓 **(Anchovy Fish Sauce)**

Adds savory taste and depth. Used in kimchi, soups, and vegetable dishes. Brands: Sempio, CJ, Chungjungone

9 *Chamgireum* 참기름 **(Sesame Oil)**

A fragrant finishing oil made from toasted sesame. Add at the end of cooking or for dipping sauces. Brands: Ottogi, Chungjungone

10 *Matsul* 맛술 **(Cooking Wine, Mirin-style)**

Softens meat and removes odors. Adds subtle sweetness to marinades. Brands: Ottogi, Chungjungone

11 *Sikcho* 식초 **(Vinegar)**

Brown rice and apple vinegar are common. Used for pickling, dipping sauces, and salads. Brands: Ottogi, Chungjungone

12 *Dajin Maneul* 다진마늘 **(Minced Garlic)**

Essential base for most Korean dishes. Often kept pre-minced in freezer or fridge.

13 *Sogeum* 소금 **(Salt)**

Includes sun-dried sea salt, fine salt, bamboo salt. Used for kimchi brining, seasoning, and traditional remedies.

14 *Pa* 파 **(Korean Scallion, Green Onion)**

White stalks for broth; green tops for garnish or flavoring. Also includes thinner variety (*jjokpa* 쪽파) often used like chives as a garnish.

15 *Chamkkae* 참깨 **(Sesame Seeds)**

Toasted or ground sesame seeds (*chamkkae* 참깨) are a pantry staple that add a nutty depth to Korean cooking. Sprinkled at the very end, they serve as both garnish and flavor enhancer. Perilla seeds (*deulkkae* 들깨) are also used, though less commonly.

1

샘표
양조간장
701
SOY SAUCE

2
샘표
한식국간장
KOREAN SOUP SOY SAUCE

6
고춧가루

7
설탕

8

남해안
멸치

3

O'Food
순창
MILD
DOENJANG

4

O'Food
순창
GOCHUJANG

5

사계절 쌈장
사계절쌈장

9

100% 통참깨
고소한
참기름
PURE ROASTED SESAME OIL

10

Food
국산 100% 생생발효
맛술

11

현미식초
YELLOW RICE RICE VINEGAR

13

소금

12

14

15

샘표
볶음참깨
ROASTED SESAME

6 Head to Toe: The Korean Way

Not sure if a "national dress code" ever really existed - but in an age of global fast fashion, where Zara, H&M, and Uniqlo fill every city block, the idea feels even more elusive.

Yet Korea, once known for its strict sartorial expectations, certainly had something close. There was a time when office workers in full suits and ties - or pencil skirts and heels - filled the streets, even in the height of monsoon season.

But things have changed. Today, unless it's a wedding or a funeral, you can show up almost anywhere in a tracksuit. The pandemic shifted norms, leaving behind not only a new sense of practicality, but a deeper craving for comfort. Plenty of Koreans have joined the global wave refusing to return to pants without elastic waistbands.

And one more thing: Korean fashion often ignores the season. On the same street in April, you might see someone in a long padded coat and another in shorts and sandals - much like a stroll through San Francisco. Seasonal boundaries blur, and individuality shows instead.

Knowing a bit about these styles also helps make historical dramas more understandable and enjoyable. From the ornate garments of historical dramas to black puffer jackets, and the omnipresent Crocs - let's take a walk through what Koreans wear—then and now.

Korean Clothing Overview
From Hanbok to Black Puffer

Hanbok 한복
Traditional Dress

Traditional Korean clothing, known today as hanbok, is built on a simple structure: the *jeogori* 저고리(upper garment) paired with either a *chima* 치마 (skirt) or *baji* 바지(trousers), often layered with *po* 포(outerwear). This form dates back to the Three Kingdoms period and continued through the Goryeo dynasty.

Toward the end of the Goryeo era, the jeogori—originally long—gradually became shorter. By the Joseon dynasty, this shorter version had become standard, shaping the silhouette most commonly associated with hanbok today.

Korean dress was also carefully adapted to the seasons: lightweight, breathable fabrics for the humid summers, and thicker materials to provide insulation in winter. Women's undergarments could include three to four layers beneath the outer garments. As the jeogori shortened in the Joseon era, an additional sash-like garment was introduced to discreetly cover the skin exposed between the jeogori and the chima.

Outerwear in Traditional Dress

In traditional Korean clothing, po broadly referred to coats and outer garments - symbols of both status and practicality. The **durumagi** 두루마기 was a common overcoat for warmth, while the dopo served as formal attire. Women sometimes added a sleeveless cape, the **sseugaechima** 쓰개치마, when going outdoors.

Traditional
Women's Accessories

daenggi 댕기 & binyeo 비녀

In traditional Korea, a woman's hairstyle and accessories signaled her stage in life. Unmarried women wore long braids tied with colorful **daenggi** 댕기 (ribbons), while married women styled their hair in a bun (**jjok** 쪽) secured with a **binyeo** 비녀 (ornamental hairpin). Both were not just decorative - they showed wealth and status.

Eunjangdo 은장도 (Silver Dagger)

A small blade often crafted from silver, worn at the waist or fastened to the breast-knot (the ribbon ties of the hanbok jacket). Both an ornamental accessory for daily dress and, in times of danger, a woman's self-defense weapon.

Norigae 노리개

Women also adorned their hanbok with norigae pendants and jewelry made from jade, gold, or silver. These items added beauty but also carried symbolic meaning, turning everyday dress into a reflection of identity.

^{The} Mad Hatters

If you think hats are just for bad hair days, Korea might change your mind.

In Joseon society, hats weren't just accessories but markers of rank, role, and ritual. The width of the brim, the material, even the chin strap - all signaled something important. Long before K-pop idols wore beanies or middle-aged ladies sported sun visors, Korea was already a hat culture.

Let's take a closer look at the headgear of the Joseon era - where fashion met philosophy.

Gat 갓 & *Gatkeun* 갓끈

Semi-transparent horsehair hat of the Joseon era: black, balanced, and philosophical.

The string and dangling beads revealed wealth and refinement - status was in the details.

Jeongjagwan 정자관

Indoor hat for scholar-officials; its layered tiers showed rank with understated elegance.

Ikseongwan 익선관

Ceremonial crown for kings and princes, with curved horn-like wings: pure power and ritual.

Jeonrip 전립

A hardened felt hat made from wild boar hide, worn in combat. High-ranking officials displayed their status through lavish decorations, while soldiers of low rank wore plain, black versions that looked austere and humble. From the width of an outer robe to the ornaments on a hat, every detail signaled rank and role.

Nambawi 남바위

Winter hat with ear flaps and neck cover, lined with fur or cotton. Practical elegance for cold days.

Gache 가채

Ornate wig for women of high status; so lavish it was said some went bankrupt or hurt their necks - for beauty.

Jokduri 족두리

A Joseon-era women's headpiece that spread from the royal court to common society. Black for daily wear, white for mourning.

Hwagwan 화관

A women's ceremonial crown of late Joseon, rooted in Silla-era headpieces. By the dynasty's end, it had become smaller in size and widely used.

▌The Royal Tailor 상의원 2014•movie

Set in the royal court of the Joseon Dynasty, this film follows two rival artisans: the traditional court tailor and a daring, rule-breaking designer. As dazzling new styles clash with palace conservatism, their rivalry unfolds not just over fashion, but also power, pride, and politics. A visual feast of hanbok history - showcasing exquisite fabrics, colors, and silhouettes that reveal both status and sentiment in Joseon society.

From
Straw Sandals to Crocs

*Before Korea had sneakers and Crocs,
it had straw sandals and silk flower shoes.*

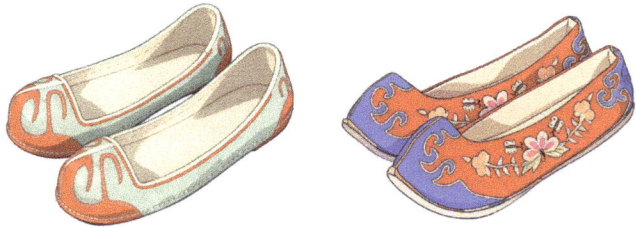

Hye 혜

Flat shoes of the Joseon era, made without raised edges or wooden soles. Taesa-hye 태사혜 for men featured the Taesa pattern on the toe and heel, while Hwa-hye 화혜 for young women were wrapped in silk and embroidered with plum blossoms or butterflies. In dramas, they often appear as unspoken tokens of affection - handmade, delicate, and heartfelt.

Mokhwa 목화

Shoes worn by civil and military officials with official robes in the Joseon era, also paired with wedding attire.

They appear frequently in historical dramas, instantly recognizable as part of courtly dress. Made with leather on the outside and sole, with hemp lining for comfort.

Jipsin 짚신

woven straw sandals for commoners. Cheap, practical, and everywhere. People even joked: "Even straw sandals come in pairs" (짚신도 짝이 있다) - a saying that captures the ache of not yet finding one's soulmate.

No Shoes in the House!

Fast Forward >>>

Crocs + Jibbitz
The post-pandemic must-haves. Once just doctors' shoes in dramas, then almost overnight, everyone wore them. Comfy, quirky, and endlessly customizable.

Slides and Socks
Today's unofficial Korean uniform. From teenagers to office workers, this combo simply says: "Comfort first."

Sneakers
The daily footwear of every generation. Once limited to the gyms, they became the go-to pairing with elastic-waist pants, a symbol of practicality. Both an urban essential and a style icon.

From straw to rubber, Korean shoes tell a story of comfort, identity, and constant change.

Modern Style 모던 스타일

From bucket hats and MLB-logo caps to soft, slouchy beanies - today's hats in Korea are all about personal flair, casual comfort, and a hint of K-idol energy.

At the same time, more formal, classic styles still hold their place among older generations - especially older men, who often finish their look with a hat that says, "I still care."

Modern Days

From *jeogori* 저고리 and *gat* 갓 to padded jackets and Crocs, Korean clothing has always balanced practicality with identity.

Black Long Puffer

The winter uniform. Worn by students, moms, dads, athletes, and K-pop idols alike. Warm, practical - and makes you look like a walking kimbap.

Training Suit & Slides

The unofficial off-duty outfit. Matching track suits in all colors, usually with a baseball cap. Effortless, yet suspiciously curated.

Couple Look

Love, mirrored. Matching outfits for couples - sometimes just the same sneakers, sometimes full head-to-toe twinsies. Cute or cringe? Depends on who's watching.

"Couple look? Cute … until it's laundry day."

K-pop Airport Look

Not just travel attire - this is a mobile runway. Oversized everything. Sunglasses indoors. And at least one fashion item that makes no practical sense whatsoever.

Fusion Hanbok 한복

Tradition, redesigned. Shorter skirts, lighter fabrics, softer tones. You'll spot them on holidays, at weddings, or in the artsy cafés of Jeonju 전주.

The Story of Park's Marriage Contract
열녀박씨 계약결혼뎐 2023-2024 • drama

Park Yeon-woo (Lee Se-young), once a virtuous wife in Joseon, suddenly finds herself in a world of denim, crop tops, and dating apps. Guided by a modern designer who takes her as his muse, she evolves into an unexpected fashion icon - turning this tale into a charming time-slip rom-com.

K-Beauty's Ecosystem:

Even in a global economic downturn, K-Beauty shows no signs of slowing. Flagships like Amorepacific continue to lead, while small labels are thriving as well. A 2025 Careet trend survey revealed that 85% of Korean Gen Z consumers now prefer smaller brands like Rom&nd, Fwee, Clio, and Naming over global luxury houses - evidence that tastes and expectations are fragmenting into ever finer niches.

This growth is powered by an ecosystem of its own: manufacturing giants such as Kolmar Korea and Cosmax driving ODM (Original Design Manufacturing) innovation; Olive Young's nationwide chain of curated beauty stores; aggressive promotion through social media; and even Daiso, the everyday discount shop, entering the low-cost cosmetics game. Together, they fuel relentless trend-setting and market segmentation. Most of all, Korea's **"kodeok"** 코덕 (cosmetic **deokhu** 덕후 meaning superfan) push the culture forward - not just as users, but as devoted enthusiasts who actively shape K-Beauty's future.

– *Careet is a trend newsletter with marketing insights for brands targeting the MZ generation.*

Skin Clinics on Every Corner

K-Beauty isn't just about cosmetics - it's a full-blown ecosystem. Many Korean brands began as OEM producers for global luxury labels, steadily building unmatched technical skill. Add to that a hyper-competitive domestic market that demands constant innovation, and you get inventions like mask sheets, BB & CC creams, essences, sleeping packs, and cushion compacts.

But beauty in Korea isn't just product-deep - it's skin-deep, too. Clear, luminous skin has been a cultural ideal long before any Western influence. Clinics stand ready on nearly every corner to help maintain that ideal. Dermatology and cosmetic procedures have become part of everyday life, powered by precision - and normalized by K-pop, social media, and a cultural ease with change. Laser toning over lunch? Totally doable. A little tweak as casually as a haircut? Why not.

And thanks to Korea's unmatched hands-on skill, plastic surgery has evolved beyond double eyelids and nose jobs to offer incredibly fine-tuned enhancements. What began as a personal choice has now grown into a full-fledged pillar of K-tourism. It's why beauty tourists now arrive with baggages and leave with bandages.

In Korea, skin care isn't a luxury - it's routine for most.

7 Creatures of K:
Beloved Beasts, Real and Imagined

From the loyal Jindo dog to the sprinting K-zombie, Korea's creatures blur the line between reality and imagination. Some live in our homes or scamper through forests; others haunt legends, dramas, and nightmares. Together, they reveal the many faces of Korea's spirit - playful, protective, mysterious, and sometimes terrifying.

Familiar

Jindotgae 진돗개 *Jindo* Dog

A native Korean breed known for fierce loyalty, sharp intelligence, and a playful yet stubborn streak. Their independence - once seen as difficult - is now a sought-after trait, making them an ideal match for modern living. Surprisingly clean and low-odor, Jindos are rising stars among indoor companions.

Practically speaking? In almost every Korean drama or film set in the countryside, you'll spot a Jindo somewhere in the background - white, fawn, brindle, or black-and-tan. Maybe they're not just in the background - they are the background.

Gorani 고라니
Water Deer

Often spotted darting across rural roads, these shy creatures look deceptively cute - until you notice the fangs. Adult males sport long, protruding canines, earning them the nickname "vampire deer." They're also infamous for their unforgettable shriek - a piercing cry that slices through the night.

With no natural predators left in Korea, the country now hosts over 70% of the world's water deer. And in pop culture, they've earned an eerie kind of fame. Remember the opening of 'Train to Busan'? A deer struck by a truck suddenly rises again - undead. Harmless at first glance. Not anymore. That was the beginning of it all.

Daramjwi 다람쥐 Squirrel

Don't let the big eyes fool you. These striped squirrels once gained global fame - with over 300,000 exported annually at their peak, all thanks to their irresistibly cute looks.

Still, they might surprise you. They've been known to hunt snakes. Yes - they're technically mice. Fierce ones. In old folktales, they symbolized saving for the future - especially for winter. Though ironically, they often forget where they hid their own acorns!

From neighbors in nature
to legends

Horangi 호랑이 Tiger

From Fearsome Beast to Folkloric Friend.

The Korean tiger, once roaming the peninsula's deep mountains, is now classified as an endangered species and no longer found in the wild. In Korea's rugged terrain, traditional folktales and children's stories often feature people running into tigers on remote mountain paths -

sometimes barely escaping danger, other times outsmarting the beast with wit and cunning.

In Korean folk paintings (*minhwa* 민화), however, the tiger rarely looks majestic. Instead, it appears clumsy, expressive, and even comical - a playful figure that gently mocks authority. In legends, the tiger could also serve as a messenger of the mountain spirit, a guardian who repays kindness, or a force that wards off misfortune.

This dual image - both fearsome and friendly - still resonates in modern culture. A recent example is Derpy from 'K-Pop Demon Hunters,' a character shaped by this tradition of the "friendly tiger."

Kkachi 까치 Magpie:
Harbinger of Guests, Friend of Tigers

In traditional Korean folk paintings, magpies often perch beside tigers in a motif called *jak-ho-do* 작호도 (magpie-and-tiger painting). Folk belief held that magpies cried out loudly when a stranger approached, which gave rise to the saying: a magpie's call means a welcome guest - or good fortune - is on the way.

But time changes affection. In modern ecology, magpies are sometimes seen as disruptive to local bird populations, and they no longer enjoy the same beloved status they once held in Korean households.

Still, the magpie remains alive in culture and art. In 'K-Pop Demon Hunters,' the so-called Galaxy Bird, Sussie - a magpie with three eyes on each side of its head - takes flight as a daring creative invention. Korean mythology does feature otherworldly birds, like the *samjok-o* 삼족오 (three-legged crow) or the *inmyeon-jo* 인면조 (human-faced bird). But a multi-eyed magpie? That's pure imagination - stretching folklore into new cosmic territory.

But some tales aren't just stories - some became guardians, watching over life itself.

Guardians & Spirits

Haetae 해태

A mythical beast with the body of a lion and a single horn on its head. Said to distinguish right from wrong, the haetae was revered as a guardian of justice in ancient Korea. You'll often spot its statues in front of palaces like Gyeongbokgung, their stern faces watching over the gates.

Today, Haetae lives on as Haechi, the official mascot of Seoul - bridging old legend with modern civic identity. The city even gave it a slogan: "Don't worry. Be Haechi."

Samshin Halmeoni 삼신할머니

The grandmother goddess of birth and fate. Samshin Halmeoni is a household deity traditionally enshrined in homes, often near the hearth. She watches over pregnancy, childbirth, and the growth of children - protecting both mother and baby. Families once made simple offerings of rice, water, or thread to honor her presence.

She isn't a figure of fear, but of gentle strength - embodying the tender balance between vulnerability and blessing that every new life carries.

Dark & Mysterious

Of course, every land of light has shadows too. Korea's creatures can trick, haunt, or even chase you.

Dokkaebi 도깨비

A mischievous goblin from Korean folklore - part trickster, part guardian. Dokkaebi aren't evil, but they love to mess with humans: playing pranks, testing character, or rewarding the worthy. They often carry a magical club that can summon anything they want - but beware, they might use it just to tease.

In the hit K-drama, 'Guardian: The Lonely and Great God', actor Gong Yoo transformed the traditional brutish goblin into a gentle, stylish immortal - brooding, handsome, and emotionally complex. A symbol of chaos, mystery, and unexpected luck, dokkaebi remain a fan favorite in Korean mythos.

Jeoseung Saja 저승사자
Grim Reaper

The jeoseung saja - the reaper of the afterlife - is a recurring figure in Korean culture, reflecting the ever-present awareness of death in the midst of life. Dressed in black, this figure symbolizes the arrival of death and guides the souls of the deceased to the afterlife. According to tradition, he appears only to those whose time has come, remaining invisible to the living.

The modern visual image of the jeoseung saja draws heavily from the iconic horror TV anthology 'The Hometown Legends (**Jeonseol-ui Gohyang** 전설의 고향)' of the late 20th century. In these portrayals, the reaper typically wears a black **gat** 갓 (traditional hat for men), a flowing black **dopo** 도포 (robe), and has a pale face with black lips - an eerie and unmistakable look.

This traditional motif was reimagined in the hit drama Guardian, where actor Lee Dong-wook played a stylish, modernized version of the reaper. And more recently, even the debut of the virtual boy band Saja Boys has drawn on this fearsome yet captivating character.

K-Zombies 좀비

From 'Train to Busan' to 'Kingdom' and 'All of Us Are Dead,' Korean zombies are fast, emotional, and fiercely collective. Less about gore, more about survival - and the collapse of social order, played out with a uniquely Korean sense of urgency.

If Western zombies crawl out of the dark, Korean zombies are different. They run - day and night - nonstop, no hesitation. Just like Koreans.

They were once your neighbors. Now, they're unsettling strangers - who strike when you try to help. But if you turn away, they stay with you... like a thorn in your conscience.

Zombie Survival Plan?

I DON'T RUN.
I PLAY DEAD.

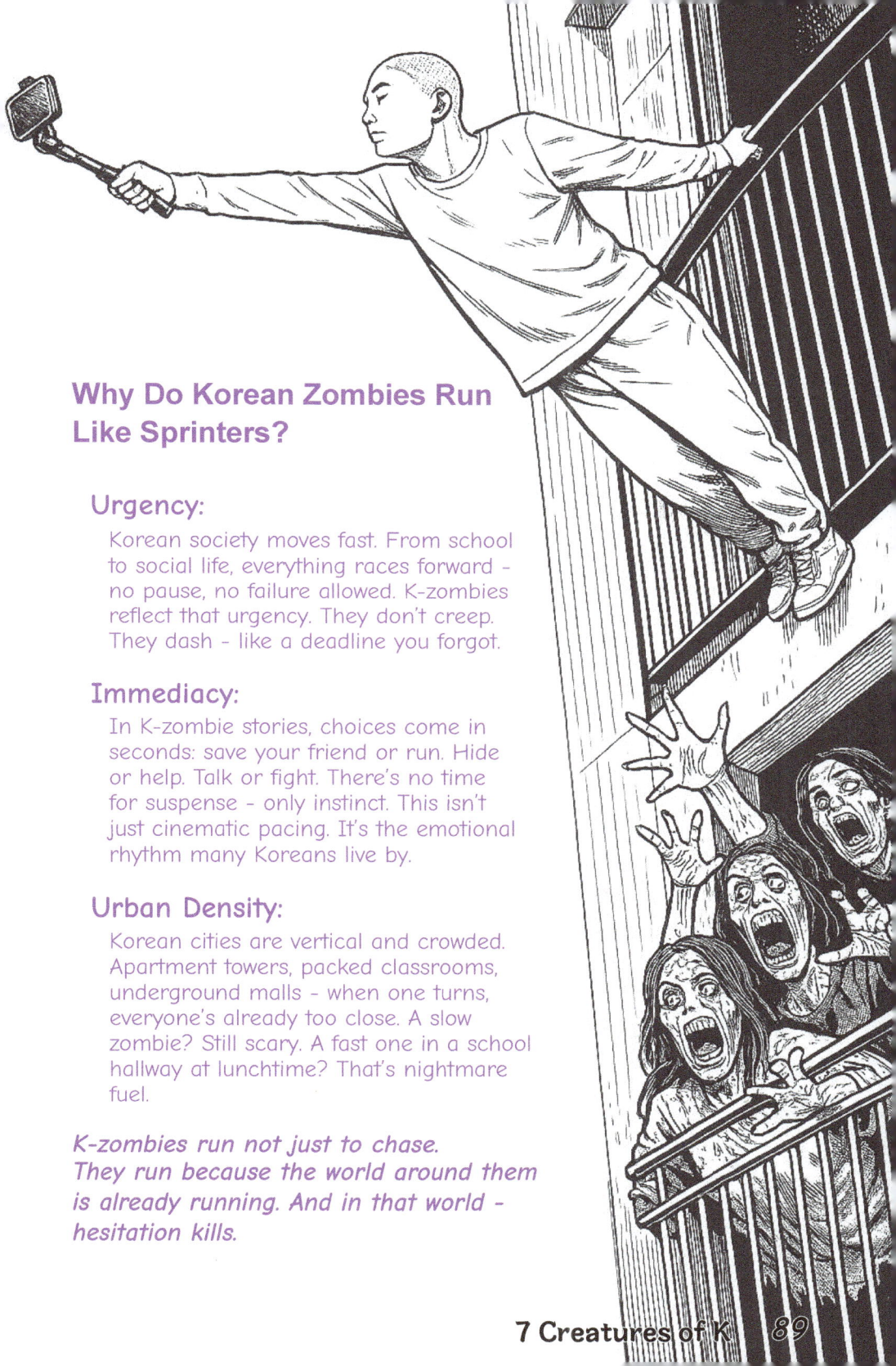

Why Do Korean Zombies Run Like Sprinters?

Urgency:

Korean society moves fast. From school to social life, everything races forward - no pause, no failure allowed. K-zombies reflect that urgency. They don't creep. They dash - like a deadline you forgot.

Immediacy:

In K-zombie stories, choices come in seconds: save your friend or run. Hide or help. Talk or fight. There's no time for suspense - only instinct. This isn't just cinematic pacing. It's the emotional rhythm many Koreans live by.

Urban Density:

Korean cities are vertical and crowded. Apartment towers, packed classrooms, underground malls - when one turns, everyone's already too close. A slow zombie? Still scary. A fast one in a school hallway at lunchtime? That's nightmare fuel.

K-zombies run not just to chase.
They run because the world around them
is already running. And in that world -
hesitation kills.

Alive 살아있다 2020 • movie

This survival thriller follows a young gamer trapped in his apartment as a sudden zombie outbreak ravages Seoul. Cut off from the world, he struggles with isolation and dwindling supplies until an unexpected neighbor sparks a fragile hope for escape.

Kingdom 킹덤 2019-2020 • drama

Set in the late Joseon Dynasty, this political-horror thriller follows a crown prince uncovering a mysterious plague turning people into the undead. Amid famine, corruption, and a collapsing kingdom, he must both battle zombies and navigate court intrigue to claim his right to the throne.

A gripping fusion of history and horror - where even the hats of Joseon steal the scene, each brim and crown shading the struggles of power, class, and survival.

Guardian: The Lonely and Great God
도깨비 2016 • drama

This fantasy romance centers on an immortal goblin who seeks release from his eternal life, and the human bride destined to end it. As he navigates fate alongside a grim reaper and a high school girl who can see the unseen, love and loss intertwine across centuries.

A sweeping tale of myth and mortality - where an elegant goblin, a handsome grim reaper, and the goddess of birth appear in strikingly modern form.

Susu's Box

Who Taught K-Zombies to Move Like That?

They don't just walk. They snap. Twist. Collapse mid-run - then spring back like broken puppets. That signature K-zombie movement - frenzied, contorted, weirdly beautiful - wasn't random. It was choreographed.

The zombies in 'Train to Busan' and 'Kingdom' were trained by Jeon Young, a dancer and choreographer with a background in bone-breaking - a street dance style built on joint isolations and unnatural contortions.

Together with his crew, Centipedz, Jeon brought a new kind of monster to the screen: not just infected, but inhumanly expressive.

Each project had its own movement style: In 'Train to Busan,' zombies flail like every muscle has gone rogue - fast, jerky, terrifying. In 'Kingdom,' they move like sleepwalkers... until they don't.

This isn't just acting. It's body horror by design performed by dancers who know exactly how to make your skin crawl.

K-zombies aren't just monsters. They're choreography in motion.

Sources: Interview with zombie choreographer Jeon Young (YouTube), Korea JoongAng Daily "How K-zombies Are Brought to Screens"

Dir. Bong's Creatures:

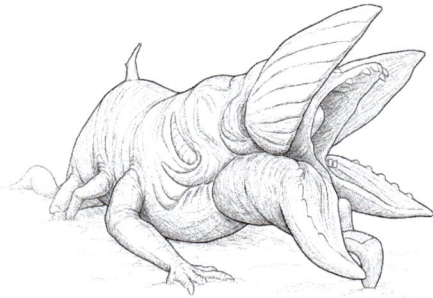

● The Han River Monster
괴물 2006 • movie

From The Host, this creature isn't just terrifying. It's a metaphor - for pollution, government failure, and the things we'd rather ignore... until they crawl out from under the bridge.

● Okja 옥자 2017 • movie

A genetically modified "super pig" raised like family - torn between love and capitalism. Endearing yet unsettling, Okja makes you ask: what (or who) are we willing to sacrifice for progress?

● Croissant Thing
미키 17 2025 • movie

This flaky, sad-eyed being became an SNS star almost overnight - especially after Bong Joon-ho was spotted hugging its plushie like a baby. In the film, it's actually an alien species called Creepers. No one knows exactly what it is. But somehow... we feel for it.

8 The Korean Codes:
Under the Surface

The emotional undercurrents of Korea - heung, tsundere warmth, anxiety, collective fatigue, and a few fading codes - shape how people speak, celebrate, protest, and even fall in love.

Another layer of this code runs deeper: the ways Koreans believe, pray, and look for meaning when life feels uncertain.

Heung 흥 as Collective Flow

Heung is pure, unfiltered joy and energy - bubbling up without warning, especially when people come together. You hear it in the chants of the Red Devils at a soccer match, or in the thunderous singalongs at concert halls.

But heung isn't just joy - it's flow. When thousands of voices rise in unison, performer and audience dissolve into one body, moving to the same rhythm. In Korea, the crowd loves to sing. *Ttechang* 떼창, the fan chorus turns concerts into communion, where music is no longer performed to you, but with you.

At its heart, heung is about participation, support, and togetherness.

— Large pro-democracy rallies often turn into concert-like gatherings —

Tsundere - like Warmth 츤데레 온기

Rough on the outside, quietly caring underneath. Think of the meme: handing over a precious gift with the words "*juwotda* 주웠다" ("Found it on the way"). A cultural wink at the way many - especially men - hide affection behind awkward delivery.

Found it
On the way.

In a way, it connects to the older Korean concept of *jeong* 정 - a deep, often wordless affection that extends even to strangers. Tsundere warmth may seem like a step back, but at its core, it's still about reaching out, even if the gesture comes wrapped in hesitation.

"Tsundere" is a Japanese slang term for a character cold at first (tsun-tsun) but later showing affection (dere-dere).

Buran 불안 Anxiety

Not always visible - but almost always there. In Korea, anxiety hums like a low background noise that never switches off. Its roots may lie in the country's painful division, but today it's more about survival itself.

In a society built on strong ethnic, linguistic, and cultural homogeneity, the pressure to stand out is intense. You're expected to outdo - to be taller, score higher, live in a pricier apartment - just to keep up. Even weekends are planned like missions, every hour accounted for.

When Squid Game hit the world, global audiences gasped at its brutality. Many Koreans, though, found it almost dull - because for them, that sense of endless competition was nothing new.

Squid Game

Season 1-3 2021-2025
Dir. Hwang Dong-hyuk

456 players, all driven into debt, gather in an arena where survival is the only currency. The pursuit of an enormous prize unfolds through children's games—Red Light, Green Light, tug-of-war, Round and Round, and many others... until the squid game itself. Yet beneath those innocent rules, brutal violence emerges, creating scenes that feel grotesque and uncanny.

The characters' trajectories are as unpredictable as the games. A pitiful gambling addict reveals unexpected humanity at the brink of death; a former winner ascends to the role of overseer; and a jaded tycoon, numb to every pleasure, plays the lethal game, for fun.

The series unfolds like a vast social experiment. Simple childhood games erupt into deadly contests, mirroring the underlying anxiety of Korean society—endless competition, a system where a single failure means elimination, and the fragile traces of humanity struggling to survive within it.

jipdan piro 집단 피로 Collective Exhaustion

"So tired, even joy feels like work."

In today's Korea, burnout isn't just personal - it's collective. Delivery meals replace family tables. *Mukbang* 먹방 (broadcasted eating show) replaces conversation. Vlogs replace hanging out.

We don't always gather. We watch.

Others eating, dating, parenting, crying - outsourced moments of living.

It's not pure disconnection. It's delegation. A society where life itself sometimes feels subcontracted out.

"My daily workout?

Watching my mutuals work out on Instagram. Emotional support counts, right?"

One more set!
Don't die, buddy!

The Outsourced Experience

Gwanchal Yeneung 관찰예능 (Observational Reality) makes outsourcing possible.

We're watching, not doing, in a world that keeps telling us to hustle...
Why do we love reality shows, mukbangs, vlogs, and reaction videos?
Because they let us feel without effort.
They offer a world that keeps moving - even when we can't.

"You eat. I'll watch."
"You travel. I'll rest."
"You feel. I'll stay here."
We're not disconnected.
We're just conserving energy.

From tender family diaries to single-life chronicles, from awkward romance to intergenerational banter, Korea's observational reality shows capture everyday life with a lens that feels both intimate and universal.

Home Alone 나 혼자 산다

What do solo celebrities do when no one's watching? We watch them eat, nap, clean, text friends - even get full medical checkups. Then we comment on them... commenting on themselves. And somehow, it's oddly satisfying.

The Return of Superman 슈퍼맨이 돌아왔다

Dads left alone with toddlers. Chaos? Sort of. Adorable? Absolutely. Raising kids is hard. Watching other people's kids? So cute. They grow fast. And somehow, their dads seem ...better.

▌Heart Pairing 하트페어링
▌Heart Signal 하트시그널
▌Single's Inferno 솔로지옥

Beautiful people, perfect lighting, and a lot of almosts. We watch the glances, the shy gestures, the quiet rivalry - and the not-so-quiet jealousy.
Who likes whom? Who will choose whom? And more importantly... why do we care so much?

▌My Ugly Duckling 미운 우리 새끼
▌My Kid's Romance 내 새끼의 연애

Celebrity moms watch their grown-up kids on TV - and narrate their every move.
We watch the moms watching their kids.
Commentary, sighs, awkward silence, laughter.
And somewhere between the jokes and the judgment, you wonder: Do we ever really grow up in our mother's eyes?

If My Ugly Duckling is about mothers observing daily life, My Kid's Romance zooms in on something even more delicate: their children's love lives. Mothers - and sometimes fathers, too - watch and react: with pride, with shock, and often with humor. It's a reminder that in Korea, romance isn't always entirely private, but often subject to family scrutiny.

Final note:
These shows aren't about big drama. They're about the tiny moments that sneak up on you - funny, familiar, and sometimes more real than real life. They let us rest, relate, and feel - without doing a thing.
But maybe that's the question, too.

Is it rest, or resignation?

Jonggyo 종교 Religion

Who Do Koreans Pray To?

For a country with no official religion, Korea is overflowing with belief - temples tucked into the hills, neon-lit churches on every corner, and shamans livestreaming *saju* 사주 (Korean astrology) and fortune-telling - and these days, even tarot readings - on YouTube. Spirituality here is layered, practical, and still evolving.

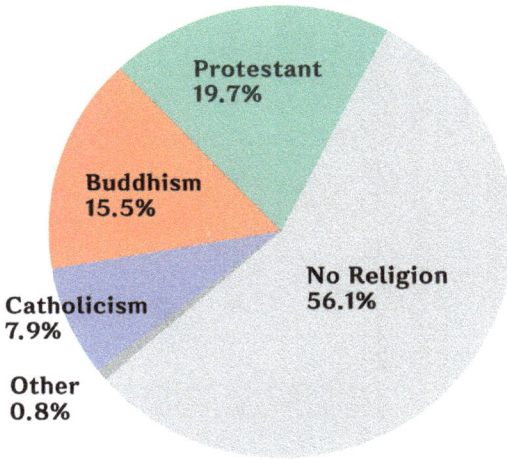

Religious Affiliation in Korea
Ministry of Culture, Sports and Tourism, Korea (2018)

● From Philosophy to Martyrdom

Confucianism arrived from China and didn't ask for faith - but for discipline. It taught how to live and how to bow, not how to pray. Yet it ruled Joseon Korea, shaping patriarchy and social hierarchy for centuries - still casting long, often burdensome shadows in everyday life.

Buddhism, rooted in the Silla dynasty, spread not through conquest but stillness - leaving behind stone Buddhas and temples folded into mountains. Even now, Buddha's Birthday is a national holiday, when cities bloom with lotus lanterns. For many, it's not about doctrine but small moments: holding your grandmother's hand at a temple, or stumbling into a shrine mid-hike, surrounded by pine and incense.

Catholicism took a very different route. Instead of arriving with missionaries, it began when Korean scholars smuggled theology books from China - embracing the faith on their own. The idea that all people were equal before God clashed with the rigid Confucian order and sparked brutal persecution. Uniquely, this was a church born from laypeople, not clergy - a rare case in global church history. In 1984, the Vatican canonized 103 Korean martyrs, recognizing their sacrifice for faith and equality. In modern Korea, Catholic churches stood at the center of democracy movements - sheltering protestors, amplifying calls for justice, and offering a moral compass.

Protestantism boomed alongside Korea's modernization. Missionary-founded schools like Yonsei and Ewha shaped the education system - opening doors not only to the elite, but also, for the first time, to women. Its message of personal salvation and energetic worship resonated with a nation eager to rebuild. For many, faith began in childhood - tagging along to summer Bible school, not out of deep belief but curiosity and community. Even today, Christianity is everywhere: flyers near subway exits, hymns from small churches, or a street sermon echoing across a busy intersection.

In pop culture, "church oppa" (**gyohoe oppa** 교회오빠) describes a clean-cut, gentle young man - less a religious label than shorthand for dependable charm.

oppa (오빠) literally means "older brother" when spoken by a female sibling, but is also widely used by women to address older male friends, boyfriends, and even young male idols.

● The Oldest Religion Never Left

For many Koreans - regardless of formal religion - prayer still means whispering to spirits. Shamanism, or **musok** 무속, predates any imported faith. It centers on the mudang - a Korean sharman, usually women, often marginalized, yet powerful. Through trance, ritual, and drumming, they connect to the spirit world - offering healing, guidance, comfort, and, at times, protection.

A **gut** 굿, the core shamanic ritual, is part theater, part therapy. There are colorful costumes, offerings, fire, dancing, and even standing barefoot on blades - a dramatic act to prove the connection to the spirit world. People still seek a **gut** 굿 for college exams, weddings, business launches - any moment when fate feels uncertain. Even now, when misfortunes pile up, people half-jokingly say:

"Do we need a **gut** 굿?"

Today, **gut** 굿 hasn't disappeared - it's evolving. Young shamans livestream rituals on TikTok. K-Pop stages borrow talismans. Supernatural dramas keep summoning ancestral fears wired deep into culture.

Shamanic Tools

방울 Bell

Spirits love sound. Bells call them - or warn them off.

부적 Talisman

Red-colored charms with ancient symbols. Burnt, buried or carried for protection

부채 Fan

Used to sweep away bad luck or invite good spirits. Also part of ritual dance.

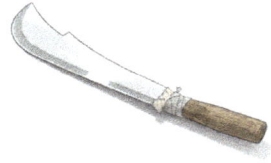

칼 Ritual Sword

Used to cut off evil energies. Often waved during a *gut* 굿 to symbolize spiritual connection.

작두 Trance Blade

Large blade that shamans stand on during trance - proof of spiritual possession.

삼지창 Trident

Symbol of divine authority. Staked in the ground to anchor energy.

Demon Hunters and Dream Portals

In 'K-Pop Demon Hunters,' shamanic tools go glam - fans spot actual *mugu* 무구 (ritual gear) on stage: swords, bells, tiger charms, red-thread spells. These aren't just props. They're cultural and spiritual symbols, reimagined as choreographed girl power.

In cinema, 'Exhuma' dives into ancestral unrest - where graves, ghosts, and Gen-Z shamans meet under the glow of Apple headphones. 'The Moon Palace' weaves fate, reincarnation, and vengeance into a dreamy cycle. And in 'Head Over Heels,' a shy boy plagued by misfortune is saved by a girl shaman-in-training - his celestial match. Together, they rewrite the stars - not through submission, but choice.

Across these stories, shamanic symbols aren't feared - they're formative. Reclaimed, repurposed, and reborn. In Korea, belief isn't about one truth. It's about coexisting with many - gods, ghosts, ancestors, and dreams, all sharing the same space.

▌The Priests 검은 사제들 2015 • movie

Catholic Exorcism and Evil Spirits A seasoned priest teams up with a fiery seminarian (played by Kang Dong-won) to save a girl possessed by a malevolent spirit. Blending Catholic ritual with Korean cinematic tension, this hit highlighted both faith and doubt in the face of the unknown.

Secret Sunshine 밀양 2007 • movie

Christian Faith and the Question of Salvation *Starring Cannes-winning actress Jeon Do-yeon and directed by novelist-turned-director Lee Chang-dong, this searing story follows a grieving mother who relocates to her late husband's hometown - only to face another unspeakable tragedy. Turning to Christianity for solace, she finds the fragile limits of forgiveness and divine grace. The film asks: can salvation ever be complete in the human realm?*

Svaha: The Sixth Finger 사바하 2019 • movie

Cult Religions and Spiritual Anxieties *Lee Jung-jae plays a pastor investigating new religious movements, only to be pulled into a chilling prophecy tied to a Buddhist sect. Mixing Christianity, Buddhism, and cult imagery, the film reflects the tangled, tense religious landscape of modern Korea.*

Exhuma 파묘 2024 • movie

Shamanism, Geomancy, and Ancestral Curses *Kim Go-eun - best known for luminous romantic roles - surprised audiences as a Converse-wearing Gen Z shaman in this blockbuster. Called to relocate a family grave, her team awakens a terrifying ancestral curse. The film shows how old rituals still ripple powerfully through today's Korea.*

Together, these films show how Korean cinema keeps circling back to faith, fear, and the unseen - sometimes for thrills, sometimes as social critique, and often as both. Whether through Christian salvation, Catholic exorcism, cult religions, or shamanistic ritual, they mirror the ways in which spiritual belief continues to shape Korean imagination today.

Fading Codes
— Nunchi, Han, and Shinpa

Some emotions don't disappear. They just soften into gentler shades. Since the Gen X era of the 1990s, emotional codes like nunchi, han, and shinpa have begun to feel at least a generation away: too indirect, too heavy, too slow for a hyper-verbal, fast-moving world. But of course - they haven't vanished.

● *Nunchi* 눈치

Once the ultimate survival skill - reading the room, the silence, the glance. Too subtle for today's quick-talking world, it has folded into modern manners: knowing when to stop talking, when not to bring a plus-one, or how to read the silence of a group chat.

● *Han* 한

A generational ache born of war, loss, and division. Once a knot in the national soul, today it feels more like history's mood - a poetic lens to understand the past, or a dramatic shorthand for lingering frustration. Think of the idiom "han-i maechida" - literally, "sorrow tied into a knot." Or more playfully:

"너 아이스크림에 *han maechyeonnya* 한 맺혔냐?"
- "Did you swear revenge on that ice cream, or what?"

Oh No!
I can't take this.
Never leave her alone...

● *Shinpa* 신파

The classic tearjerker. The trembling voice. The villain finally getting what they deserve. Borrowed from Japanese theater but shaped by Korea's own rhythms, shinpa was once moving and comforting. To Gen Z and Millennials - raised on irony and memes - it can feel overdone, sometimes even funny. And yet, with the retro wave of K-content, shinpa is creeping back. Not in the old form, but as a knowing wink: a too-sweet reunion, a scene that dares to care - without irony.

Something fades, yet others persist.

9 K-Pop: All in One Bowl

Susu asks, Is K-Pop a Genre?

Britpop. J-Pop. K-Pop. At first glance, it sounds like just another pop with a passport.

But spend five minutes watching a K-Pop stage, and you'll know - it's something else.

K-Pop isn't just music. If K-Pop had to be defined in one word, it would be convergence. It's performance, choreography, costumes, visual storytelling, behind-the-scenes content, viral moments, and fan rituals - all tightly choreographed, down to the last wink.

Like Korea's own bibimbap, it's everything in one bowl - music, visuals, fan culture, and industry, all mixed into one genre-busting experience.

Now let's take a close look at the K of K-Pop

What, then, makes K-Pop feel different from pop elsewhere? Let's start with the features that stand out most clearly.

Distinctive Features

First of all, the most striking musical trait is **genre fusion.**
K-Pop tracks effortlessly blend pop, hip-hop, EDM, R&B, disco, house, and even traditional Korean or world rhythms. There's no genre hierarchy - what matters is impact. One song might carry a trap verse, a disco chorus, and a folk-style bridge. This hybrid or fusion formula creates spectacles with broad appeal.

And lyrics are absolutely **youth-centric.**
K-Pop's lyrics (and the music itself) are steeped in the DNA of youth. Not only are the groups themselves made up of young members, but the lyrics mirror the concerns and emotions of their generation. The dominant trend leans toward insecure identities, growth, first loves, and the encouragement to keep moving forward. Rather than being purely confessional, K-Pop lyrics are dialogic, creating an exchange between stage and audience.

The musical energy reflects this same youthful drive. Major keys, energetic beats, and confidence-boosting vibes dominate.

A finely tuned arrangement also stands out.

The music is more than sound - it is structured around part distribution (who sings or raps which lines) within groups and choreography-aware composition. It is also built on a hook-centric design optimized for TikTok challenges. Rap lines, power vocals, and chorus builds are split strategically across members. The music itself leaves space for choreography: beats pause for moves, bridges serve as visual climaxes. Songs revolve around catchy hooks, both musical and lyrical, ensuring quick recognition and easy sharing. This is clearly a design with social platforms in mind.

K-Pop is made not just to be heard - but to be looped, danced to, and shared online, often together with fans. The secret that makes this possible can be summed up in one word: convergence.

@K-POP ROCKS
연습은 힘들어 Everyday #LoveUrself
#Yeonseupsaeng #idol #choreography

Convergence

Team-Based Convergence

Of course, all music is collaborative. But in K-Pop the scale of collaboration is different. Songs are written with choreography, part distribution, and international audiences already in mind, making the process resemble a full production house more than the work of a single artist.

Media Convergence

K-Pop is designed for the TikTok and YouTube era. Songs are visual from the outset - crafted with performance, story, and viral potential in mind. A K-Pop comeback isn't just an audio drop - it's a full-spectrum media event: teaser photos, dance practices, music videos, variety shows, and interactive livestreams.

Fandom & Marketing Convergence

K-Pop fandom is anything but passive - fans edit fancams, launch trends, stream songs in waves, and organize campaigns. It's a marketing ecosystem fueled by active, global participation.

From stream to scream - K-Pop hooks you in. Start with a music app, end up in a concert arena, lightstick in hand. Albums, merch, paid fan messages, and more: it's convergence beyond sound, a system designed with the synergy of related industries in mind.

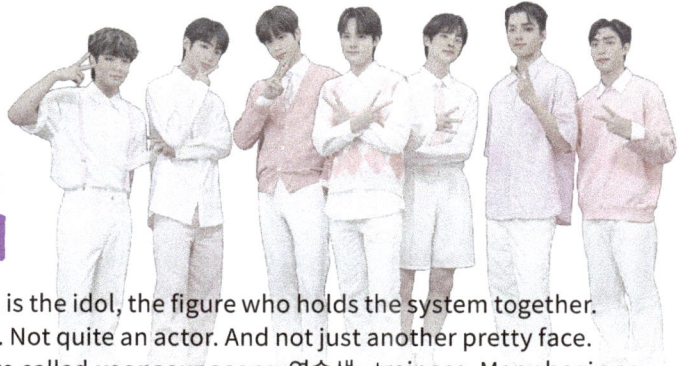

At the Center :
The Idol

At the center of it all is the idol, the figure who holds the system together. Not quite a pop star. Not quite an actor. And not just another pretty face. Before debut, they're called **yeonseupsaeng** 연습생 - trainees. Many begin as teens, training for years not just in music and dance, but also in languages, etiquette, and media literacy. It's serious business. Idols are artists, brands, and sometimes walking mythologies. Groups are engineered for synergy - every role is calculated: rap lines, main vocals, lead dancers, and even the **maknae** 막내 (the adorable and talented youngest).

Idol fans don't just listen. They analyze, archive, advocate, protest against the mistreatment of members, and celebrate. More than fandom - it's devotion. They grow with the team, witnessing every moment like family. And they are also half-specialists. In Netflix's 'Hospital Playlist: A Time Called You,' the fictional idol group Highboyz appeared with the song "That Day Will Come". Global fans instantly recognized it as "second-gen K-Pop" in feel, proving how deeply fans understand subtle formula shifts across generations.

Not all that glitters is gold—K-Pop shines, but it also casts long shadows.

Trainees, many still teenagers, endure years of grueling training - strict diets, endless rehearsals, and constant evaluation. A lucky few debut; many more leave school behind, only to be pushed back into the world with little preparation.

Even successful idols live under pressure. Their carefully curated lives on social media inspire millions, but also set unrealistic standards of beauty and success.

Creatively, the tightly systemized industry sometimes blurs the line between inspiration and imitation. And when formulas dominate, the very things we look for in art - fresh colors, new risks, and surprise - can slowly fade away.

For global fans,
K-Pop idols might be almost virtual.

The first connection happens on screen or on stage: through music videos, livestreams, then concerts worldwide. The second unfolds in real space, when fans visit the streets, cafés, and filming sites linked to their stars. In this way, K-Pop not only fills playlists, but also maps Korea itself into a lived, shared stage.

In the end, K-Pop is not just a genre - it's a shared stage where music, industry, and fans converge.

Some Songs to Know

- ### Into the New World 다시 만난 세계 — Girls' Generation

  A bright debut track that became an unexpected protest anthem - chanted at rallies and candlelight vigils as a new generation's song of hope.

- ### Boombayah 붐바야 — BLACKPINK

  A debut that roared onto the global stage. Hard-hitting beats, fierce choreography, and a "girl crush" image that redefined K-pop's reach. Its cameo in Netflix's 'Wednesday' reminded the world that Boombayah still thunders years later.

- ### IDOL 아이돌 — BTS

  A swirling blend of tradition and futurism. Onstage: ancestral drums, hanbok silhouettes, and neon spectacle. Message? "You can't stop me lovin' myself."

- ### Sodapop 소다팝 — Saja Boyz (K-Pop Demon Hunters)

  A fictional group, but the song screams K-Pop. Light, bouncy, and catchy - Sodapop shows how even in English, French, or Spanish, some songs just feel unmistakably K-Pop.

Susu's Box

Global Idols, How Korean for K?

Once upon a time, K-Pop idols were unmistakably Korean. They were scouted at street corners in Seoul, trained in mirrored studios for years, and debuted with songs that spoke Korean lyrics first, English choruses later. But in the past decade, something changed. The K in K-Pop began to travel - stretching beyond borders, adopting faces, voices, and accents from across the globe.

Today, when you watch a K-Pop music video, you might find members introducing themselves in Japanese, Chinese, Thai, or English before bowing in Korean. Entire groups are built for overseas markets, and in some cases, the majority of members aren't even Korean. Yet fans rarely hesitate to call it K-Pop. So here's the riddle we're left with: How Korean is K-Pop, when its idols come from everywhere else?

WayV: The China Sub-Unit

Consider WayV, the China-based unit of NCT, launched in 2019 by SM Entertainment. The group is composed mostly of Chinese members, designed for a Chinese-speaking market. They release Mandarin-language tracks, appear on Chinese shows, and target regional tours. Still, their training, their performance style, and their polished visual storytelling all echo the same playbook as their Seoul-based counterparts. It's K-Pop in Chinese twist.

NiziU: K-Pop in Japanese

Take NiziU, the nine-member girl group formed in Japan in 2020 through a local audition program run by JYP Entertainment. Every member is Japanese. They sing primarily in Japanese. And yet, watch their choreography, their styling, their teaser rollout, and you'll know instantly - it's K-Pop. The system was K, even if the voices weren't.

Katseye: The Global K-Pop Group debuted in the U.S.

Then there's Katseye, formed in 2024 through a survival audition program in partnership with HYBE. There's only one Korean member out of six. Their accents, their cultural references, their family backgrounds are different. But their debut felt familiar. Fans immediately recognized the teaser structure, the choreography intensity, and the cinematic storytelling of the music videos. It didn't matter where they came from; the moment they stepped on stage, the K was already there.

Major agencies like HYBE, JYP, SM, and YG have consistently scouted talent and prepared localization strategies in markets such as the United States, Japan, China, and across Southeast Asia. JYP and HYBE have also expanded into Latin America. Most recently, HYBE established a local subsidiary in India, aiming to enter that market. These companies not only support the local activities of existing artists but also hold auditions in different countries and build training systems that adapt the K-formula to local contexts - discovering and nurturing new artists around the globe.

So what, exactly, defines the "K"? Perhaps the truest answer is: Korean in system, global in reach.

Mini
Glossary of K-Pop

- ## Survival Audition 서바이벌 오디션
  TV competitions where trainees fight for a debut spot. Many iconic groups - like Wanna One and I.O.I from Produce 101, and later ENHYPEN from I-Land - originated from these shows.

- ## *suk-so* 숙소 Dorm
  Shared living space for idols. Fans often imagine the daily chaos of multiple members under one roof.

- ## Position 포지션
  A member's assigned role: center, main vocal, sub vocal, rapper, dancer, visual, or *maknae* 막내 (the youngest).

- ## *choe-ae* 최애 Bias
  Your absolute favorite member.
  chae-ae 차애 means your "second favorite."

- ## *eungwon-bong* 응원봉 Lightstick
  A group's official glowing stick, waved by fans at concerts to create a "light ocean." Each design reflects the team's identity - shapes, colors, and symbols that make it instantly recognizable and strengthen the bond between idols and fans. At large venues, Bluetooth control can sync thousands of sticks into one dazzling, coordinated display.

  In Korea, lightsticks once appeared beyond concerts - raised during candlelight protests as symbols of democracy, when fans brought out what they cherished most.

- ## *hoesa* 회사 or *gihoeksa* 기획사
  ### - Entertainment company

  Behind the group - handling training, music, and promotions. Think HYBE, JYP, SM, or YG.

- ***eum-bang*** 음방 **Music Show**

  Weekly TV programs like M Countdown, Inkigayo, and Music Bank, where idols perform, promote new songs, and compete for #1 (mostly by fan vote).

- ***jo-gong*** 조공 **Fan Support**

  Gifts fans send to idols - coffee trucks, snack packs, or even luxury goods - to cheer them on during busy schedules.

- ***yeok-jo-gong*** 역조공 **Idol Support**

  When idols return the love - buying fans snacks, drinks, lunchboxes, or small goods at fan meetings or concerts, often as a token of gratitude.

- **Bubble** 버블

  A paid subscription app where idols send private-like messages to fans. It feels one-on-one - even though it isn't.

- ***eungwon-beop*** 응원법 **Fan Chant**

  Synchronized cheers shouted by fans during live performances. Each group has its own chant - usually calling every member's name in rhythm with the song.

10 Korean Language:
How It's Different from English

In 2023, Korean was ranked the 7th most studied foreign language in the world - according to Duolingo's 2024 report.

So, is it hard to learn?

When it comes to the writing system, the answer is: not really. Hangeul, the Korean alphabet, is famously logical and compact. Back in the 15th century, the Hunminjeongeum - the royal proclamation that introduced Hangeul - claimed that a wise person could learn it in a morning, and even a fool could master it in ten days.

Originally, Hangeul had 28 letters, but today 24 are in common use. In recognition of its cultural significance, it was inscribed on UNESCO's Memory of the World Register in 1997.

That's the alphabet. But what about the language itself?
What makes Korean tricky, especially for English speakers?

King Sejong 세종대왕
— Creator of Hangeul

Hangeul in a Nutshell

Hangeul is an alphabet system that works like Lego blocks, combining to form letters and sounds. Let's start by looking at the vowels - the core building pieces.

Vowels

Primary Elements

Vowels (*moeum* 모음) come from three cosmic symbols: From these three, all 21 vowels (10 basic + 11 extended) were created.

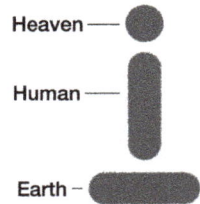

Heaven ——

Human ——

Earth —

How Vowels Sound

It sounds light or heavy, open or pulled back.

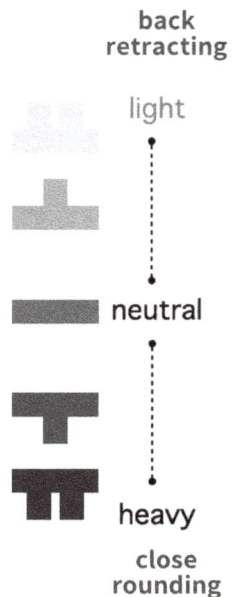

retracting ·······► neutral ◄······· open

back
retracting

light

neutral

heavy

close
rounding

116

All Korean Vowels

Derived from three primary elements, there are 10 basic and 11 extended vowels in total.

ㅏ	ㅑ	ㅓ	ㅕ	ㅗ	ㅛ	ㅜ	ㅠ	ㅡ	ㅣ
a	ya	eo	yeo	o	yo	u	yu	eu	i

ㅐ	ㅒ	ㅔ	ㅖ	ㅘ	ㅝ	ㅢ
ae	yae	e	ye	wa	wo	ui

ㅙ	ㅞ
wae	we

ㅚ	ㅟ
oe	wi

Vowel Confusion: A Common Struggle

Korean vowels sit differently in the mouth. Even native speakers sometimes confuse 'ㅐ' [ɛ] and 'ㅔ' [e] - so don't panic if you do.

For English speakers, 'ㅜ' [u] and 'ㅗ' [o] can be tricky. But the hardest one by far? 'ㅡ' **[ɯ] (eu, written as 으)**

> To pronounce 'ㅡ' (으):
>
> Start with 'oo' (as in boot),
>
> Spread your lips flat (not round),
>
> Push the sound further back in your mouth.

It should feel tighter, narrower, and more closed than anything in English.

Consonants

Base Consonants

Base consonants (*jaeum* 자음) were modeled after the shape of the speech organs: ㄱ (tongue root), ㄴ (tongue tip), ㅁ (lips), ㅅ (teeth), ㅇ (throat). All other consonants were derived from these five.

tongue	tongue	lips	teeth	throat
ㄱ	ㄴ	ㅁ	ㅅ	ㅇ

Basic Consonants

Altogether, here are 14 basic consonants in modern Korean. Some were formed by adding extra strokes to the base shapes, reflecting aspiration or other phonetic features of the sounds.

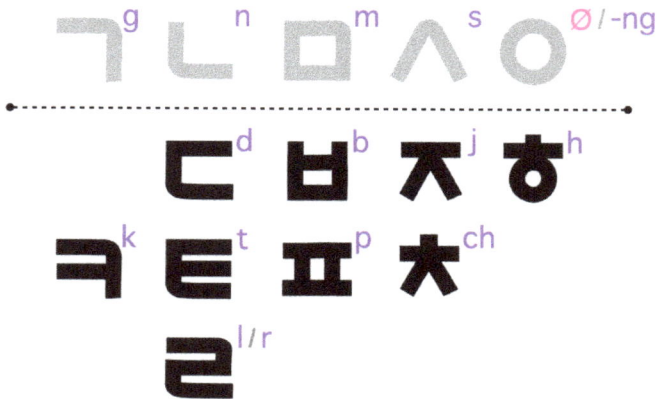

ㄱ g   ㄴ n   ㅁ m   ㅅ s   ㅇ Ø / -ng

ㄷ d   ㅂ b   ㅈ j   ㅎ h

ㅋ k   ㅌ t   ㅍ p   ㅊ ch

ㄹ l / r

Double Consonants

In addition to the 14 basics, Korean has five double consonants (ㄲ, ㄸ, ㅃ, ㅆ, ㅉ). They are tense sounds - like pressing the consonant more firmly with extra tension.

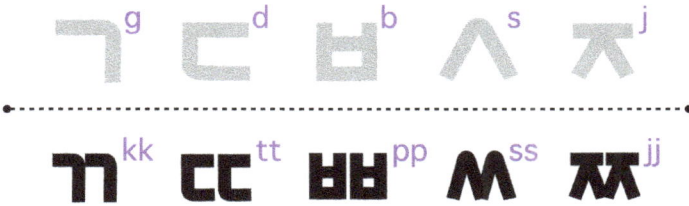

ㄱ ^g ㄷ ^d ㅂ ^b ㅅ ^s ㅈ ^j

ㄲ ^{kk} ㄸ ^{tt} ㅃ ^{pp} ㅆ ^{ss} ㅉ ^{jj}

Phonological Differences
3-way consonant distinction

Korean consonants fall into three types: plain, tense, and aspirated.

Tense consonants (ㄲ, ㄸ, ㅃ, ㅆ, ㅉ) have no equivalent in English.

Aspirated consonants (ㅋ, ㅌ, ㅍ, ㅊ) exist in English, but in Korean they're pronounced with a stronger burst of air.

Type	Examples	Description
plain	ㄱ, ㄷ, ㅂ, ㅈ	ㄱ = like **g** in gain
tense	ㄲ, ㄸ, ㅃ, ㅉ	ㄲ = a **tighter**, **stronger k**, no puff of air (no exact English equivalent)
aspirated	ㅋ, ㅌ, ㅍ, ㅊ	ㅋ = like **k** in cake, with a clear puff of air

Limited Fricatives

Korean has very few fricatives, so some English sound pairs "collapse" into one Korean consonant.

For example, fine vs. pine or van vs. ban may sound the same to Korean ears.

English	Often Collapsed in Korean	Example Mapping
f / p	→ ㅍ	fan ≈ 팬 (paen)
v / b	→ ㅂ	van ≈ 밴 (baen)
th / d	→ ㄷ	this ≈ 디스 (diseu)

Consonant "ㅇ" is special

When it comes at the beginning of a syllable, it is silent and only the vowel is pronounced. (ㅏ = 아) But when it appears at the end, it is pronounced like the English "ng" in "king." (강 [gang])

The Four Lost Letters

Four original letters - ·, ㅿ, ㆁ, and ㆆ - are no longer in use. · was a middle vowel, similar to a sound between "a" and "uh", ㅿ was a [z] sound, ㆁ marked "ng" at the beginning of a syllable, and ㆆ indicated a debated glottal stop. If they had survived, Korean pronunciation might have been even richer.

Syllable

To form a syllable, there must be at least one consonant and one vowel, with an optional final consonant.

When combined, consonants and vowels stack neatly into blocks:

Korean syllables are built from compact, Lego-like blocks:

Syllable block rules

Consonant **+ V**owel

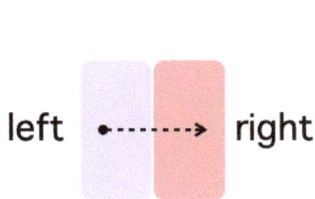

left ← - - - → right

top
↓
down

ㄱ | ㅏ   가   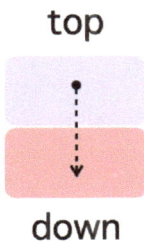   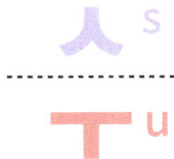

g | a   ga   u   su

gasu 가수 - singer

Syllable block rules

Consonant + **V**owel + **F**inal consonant (받침)

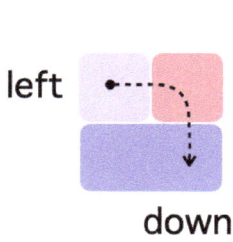

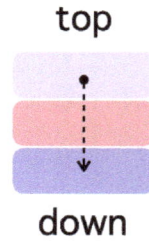

left · · · · down

top · · · down

ㅅ s ㅏ a
ㄹ r ㅁ m

삶
sam

ㅇ ∅
ㅛ yo
ㅇ ng

용
yong

sam 삶 - life

yong 용 - dragon

122

No Letter Stands Alone

You can't have a vowel or a consonant standing alone.

ah: ㅏ (x) → needs a placeholder: 아 (o)

gada: ㄱ다 (x) → needs a vowel to form a syllable: 가다 (o)

Consonant clusters like str- or chr- don't exist in Korean.

strike → 스-트-라-이-크 (seu-teu-ra-i-keu)

Chris → 크-리-스 (keu-ri-seu)

What's one syllable in English often stretches into two or three in Korean.

How Final Consonants sound

Korean syllables may end in a final consonant using all consonants and even double consonants, but in actual pronunciation only seven sounds are possible: ㄱ, ㄴ, ㄷ, ㄹ, ㅁ, ㅂ, and ㅇ. This is called the "seven final consonants rule."

Spelling vs. Pronunciation

밖 → 박

닭 → 닥

삶 → 삼

Compact, linguistically precise, and logical - Hangeul is also remarkably adaptable to the digital age. Its block-based structure almost anticipates binary thinking, making it surprisingly at home in modern computing environments.

Syntactic Differences

Korean sentences end with the verb (S + O + V), unlike English where the verb follows the subject.

And in Korean, suffixes are essential - they work like glue, holding sentences together. For English speakers, this system of endings often feels tricky, since so much meaning is hidden in those little blocks.

Word Order: Subject + Object + Verb

나는 너를 사랑**해** → I love you

나는 너를 사랑**했어** → I loved you

나는 너를 사랑**할래** → I want to love you

하다 (to do) is like a Lego base. It morphs into **해, 했어, 할래** depending on the context.

This works because Korean is agglutinative - meaning it is built block by block with particles and endings.

The Power of Particles

Particles aren't just grammar - they shape nuance. By changing a single particle, you can shift meaning:

Sentence	Translation
나**는** 너를 좋아한다.	I like you. (neutral)
나**만** 너를 좋아한다.	Only I like you.
나**도** 너를 좋아한다.	I like you, too.
나**조차** 너를 좋아한다.	Even I like you.

Korean Particles You'll See Everywhere

Particle	Function	Example	Meaning
은 / 는	topic marker	지민**은** 학교에 갔어	As for Jimin, he went to school.
이 / 가	subject marker	지민**이** 학교에 갔어	Jimin went to school. (focus on Jimin)
을 / 를	object marker	밥**을** 먹었어	(I) ate rice.
에	time place direction	학교**에** 갔어	went to school
에서	location of action	학교**에서** 공부했어	studied at school
도	also / too	지민**도** 학교에 갔어	Jimin also went to school.
만	only	지민**만** 학교에 갔어	Only Jimin went to school.
조차	even	지민**조차** 학교에 갔어	Even Jimin went to school.

Particles in Two Forms

Some Korean particles come in two forms, depending on whether the noun ends with a final consonant (받침) or not. This helps the sentence flow more smoothly in pronunciation.

Topic (은/는) → 나는 / 지민은 (Jimin은) vs. 지민이는 (Jimin이+는)

Subject (이/가) → 내가 / 지민이+가 → 지민이가 (tricky but easier to say)

Object (을/를) → 나를 / 지민을

Honorifics: Speaking with Respect

Korean uses a level-based system of politeness, often built into the verb endings - and sometimes even the nouns. Which form you use depends on age, status, and closeness between the speaker and listener.

The good news? You don't need to memorize all the extremes. In modern Korea, excessively formal or rude forms are rarely used. When in doubt, go one step more polite. It's safer that way.

Saying Hello in Korean – Levels of Politeness

Korean Expression	Romanization	When to Use
안녕	*annyeong*	With close friends, peers, younger people (informal)
안녕하세요	*annyeonghaseyo*	Everyday polite speech (safe, neutral, widely used)
안녕하십니까	*annyeonghasimnikka*	Very formal (used in interviews, news, military, announcements)

Saying Goodbye in Korean – Depending on Who Leaves

Korean Expression	Romanization	When to Use
안녕히 가세요	*annyeonghi gaseyo*	To someone **leaving** (you are staying) – polite
안녕히 계세요	*annyeonghi gyeseyo*	To someone **staying** (you are leaving) – polite
잘 가	*jal ga*	Casual, to a friend or younger person who is **leaving**
잘 있어	*jal isseo*	Casual, to a friend or younger person who is **staying**

Note: *gyesida* 계시다 is the honorific form of *itda* 있다, used when referring to someone respected.

Notice how the verb ending gets longer - and more respectful - as you go down the list.

Closing Note : Here we've looked at some of the most distinctive features of Korean from the perspective of an English speaker. Korean may feel tricky at first. But with Hangeul's logic and the rhythm of particles and endings, it soon turns from strange to intuitive. And that's where the real fun begins.

Susu's Box

Family Titles - Used Beyond Family

In Korean, family terms spill far beyond family. You'll hear eonni, oppa, imo, or samchon not only at home but also in cafés, shops, and even workplaces. They signal not just kinship, but age, gender, and a sense of closeness.

However, these are casual expressions and are not used in formal or highly polite situations.

Term	Literal Meaning	Social Usage
언니 **eonni**	Older sister (by women)	Used for women in general, or stylish/pretty women regardless of age - even strangers. Ex: shopkeepers calling out to passing women.
오빠 **oppa**	Older brother (by women)	Used for older guys to express closeness - sometimes romantic. Also used for celebs at concerts, regardless of age.
이모 **imo**	Maternal aunt	Warmly used for older women (even if younger) at shops/restaurants. Not literal.
삼촌 **samchon**	Paternal uncle	Used for middle-aged men - delivery workers, vendors, or shopkeepers. Friendly and casual.
막내 **maknae**	Youngest sibling	Refers to the youngest in a group - by age or feel. Common in offices, friend groups, and K-Pop teams.

The Mimetic Words that Feel Alive

Korean is full of sound-imitating and movement/feeling-imitating words. They're not just for kids - you'll find them in daily conversation, webtoons, even beauty ads!

Here are a few that sound as cute as they feel:

Expression	Meaning / Vibe
빨리빨리 *ppalli-ppalli*	Literally quick quick, now famous worldwide as the motto of Korea's hustle culture
버둥버둥 *beo-doong beo-doong*	Flailing or wriggling helplessly. It can also carry a lighter nuance of idling or fidgeting about with nothing to do.
반짝반짝 *ban-jjak ban-jjak*	Sparkling / twinkling (eyes, stars, clean floors!).
두근두근 *du-geun du-geun*	Heart beating fast (from love, nerves, or excitement).
사각사각 *sagak-sagak*	The crisp, crunchy sound like stepping on fresh snow, chewing on snacks, or writing with a pencil on a paper.
말랑말랑 *mal-lang mal-lang*	Soft, squishy, and bouncy - like a marshmallow, steamed bun, or fresh rice cake.

Your cheeks are so mal-lang mal-lang 말랑말랑!

Hearing that makes me du-geun du-geun 두근두근!

Forbidden Dream 천문 2019 • movie

A historical drama about King Sejong - creator of Hangeul - and Jang Yeong-sil, a brilliant scientist born a commoner. Though the narrative centers on the making of astronomical instruments, it also captures Sejong's radical vision: that ordinary people should be able to read the heavens and their own language. Here, Sejong emerges not only as a monarch but as a revolutionary mind who defied privilege to empower his people.

MAL·MO·E 말모이 The Secret Mission 2019 • movie

Set during the Japanese colonial era, this film follows the members of the Korean Language Society who risk their lives to compile the first Korean dictionary. As they gather dialects from across the country, the story reveals a powerful truth: protecting words is the same as protecting identity.

Korean Writers:
5 Novelists & 2 Poets

――――――――――― **Novelists** ―――――――――――

Han Kang 한강 1969 -
"Why is the world so violent, and yet so beautiful?"
—Nobel Lecture—
- Human Acts 소년이 온다
- The Vegetarian 채식주의자
- The White Book 흰

Jeong You-jeong 정유정 1966 -
I was my father's executioner. —Seven Years of Darkness—
- Seven Years of Darkness 7년의 밤
- The Good Son 종의 기원
- 28 28

Bae Suah 배수아 1965 -
Dreams have no entrance, just as they have no exit.
—Unfold Night and Day—
- Nowhere to Be Found 철수
- Untold Night and Day 알려지지 않은 밤과 하루
- A Greater Music 에세이스트의 책상

Cheon Myeong-kwan 천명관 1964 -
To her, pain was nothing more than an occurrence inside herself. Never anyone else's fault. —Whale—
- Whale 고래
- Homecoming 퇴근
- Modern Family 고령화가족

Hwang Jungeun 황정은 1976 -
Where does the mind reside? d believed it was in the jaw— because her jaw hurts. —Didi's umbrella—
- One Hundred Shadows 百의 그림자
- Didi's Umbrella 디디의 우산
- I'll go on 계속해보겠습니다

Note - All titles mentioned are available on Goodreads.

--- **Poets** ---

Kim Hyesoon 김혜순 1955 -

From the place where no reply can be sent, a letter will come. —Autobiography of Death—

- Autobiography of Death 죽음의 자서전
- Phantom Pain Wings 날개 환상통
- Poor Love Machine 불쌍한 사랑기계

Kim Haengsook 김행숙 1970 -

It's all trivial now, she will say through tears. Caress her. A good friend is gentle indeed. —Adolescence—

- Human Time: Selected Poem (Selected from five volumes of poetry)

In Korean only:

『사춘기』 Adolescence
『이별의 능력』 The Ability to Part
『에코의 초상』 Portrait of Echo

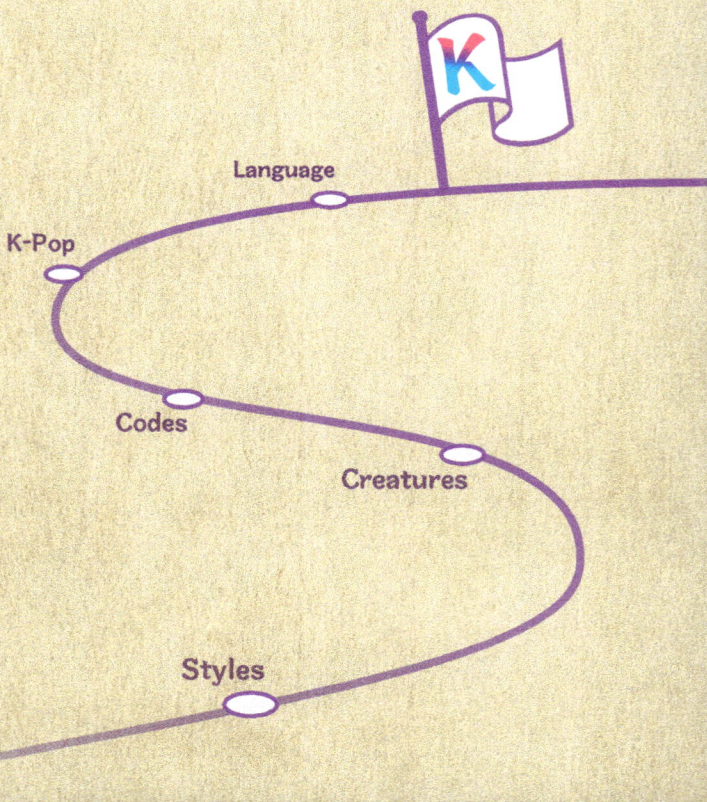

K

Language

K-Pop

Codes

Creatures

Styles

That's our stroll for now.

Thank you for walking alongside me and Susu.

I hope you've discovered a small, intimate K-moment for yourself.

See you in the next alley.

Cheers,
Min & Susu

I can't say the words. Cue the heart!

Consonant-Vowel
Combination Charts

	ㅏ a	ㅑ ya	ㅓ eo	ㅕ yeo	ㅗ o	ㅛ yo	ㅜ u	ㅠ yu	ㅡ eu	ㅣ i
ㄱ g	가	갸	거	겨	고	교	구	규	그	기
ㄴ n	나	냐	너	녀	노	뇨	누	뉴	느	니
ㄷ d	다	댜	더	뎌	도	됴	두	듀	드	디
ㄹ r	라	랴	러	려	로	료	루	류	르	리
ㅁ m	마	먀	머	며	모	묘	무	뮤	므	미
ㅂ b	바	뱌	버	벼	보	뵤	부	뷰	브	비
ㅅ s	사	샤	서	셔	소	쇼	수	슈	스	시
ㅇ *	아	야	어	여	오	요	우	유	으	이
ㅈ j	자	쟈	저	져	조	죠	주	쥬	즈	지
ㅊ ch	차	챠	처	쳐	초	쵸	추	츄	츠	치
ㅋ k	카	캬	커	켜	코	쿄	쿠	큐	크	키
ㅌ t	타	탸	터	텨	토	툐	투	튜	트	티
ㅍ p	파	퍄	퍼	펴	포	표	푸	퓨	프	피
ㅎ h	하	햐	허	혀	호	효	후	휴	흐	히

ㄱ g | ㅏ a → 가 ga   ㅅ s / ㅜ u → 수 su

	ㅐ ae	ㅒ yae	ㅔ e	ㅖ ye	ㅘ wa	ㅙ wae	ㅚ oe	ㅝ wo	ㅞ eu	ㅟ wi	ㅢ ui
ㄱ g	개	걔	게	계	과	괘	괴	궈	궤	귀	긔
ㄴ n	내	냬	네	녜	놔	놰	뇌	눠	눼	뉘	늬
ㄷ d	대	댸	데	뎨	돠	돼	되	둬	뒈	뒤	듸
ㄹ r	래	럐	레	례	롸	뢔	뢰	뤄	뤠	뤼	릐
ㅁ m	매	먜	메	몌	뫄	뫠	뫼	뭐	뭬	뮈	믜
ㅂ b	배	뱨	베	볘	봐	봬	뵈	붜	붸	뷔	븨
ㅅ s	새	섀	세	셰	솨	쇄	쇠	숴	쉐	쉬	싀
ㅇ *	애	얘	에	예	와	왜	외	워	웨	위	의
ㅈ j	재	쟤	제	졔	좌	좨	죄	줘	줴	쥐	즤
ㅊ ch	채	챼	체	쳬	촤	쵀	최	춰	췌	취	츼
ㅋ k	캐	컈	케	켸	콰	쾌	쾨	쿼	퀘	퀴	킈
ㅌ t	태	턔	테	톄	톼	퇘	퇴	퉈	퉤	튀	틔
ㅍ p	패	퍠	페	폐	퐈	퐤	푀	풔	풰	퓌	픠
ㅎ h	해	햬	헤	혜	화	홰	회	훠	훼	휘	희

101 Titles from 2020 Onward
A Curated List of K-Dramas & Films

What's inside:

> *101 picks—from global hits to hidden gems—arranged in alphabetical order by English title.*

Icons: ■ = drama / □ = film

How we chose them:

> *Not a ranking, but a curated mix. Think buzzy series, talked-about films, and cultural touchstones that landed anywhere from fine to phenomenal.*

Where to watch:

> *Netflix, Disney+, & Apple TV (availability may shift). Unless otherwise noted, titles are available on Netflix.*

Big picture:

> *This isn't everything - it's more like a playlist for exploration. A way to dip into Korea's screen culture, one story at a time.*

□ **#Alive #살아있다 2020 Horror, Zombie / 98 min / TV-MA**
Trapped in a locked-down apartment complex, two survivors struggle against the zombie outbreak.
Yoo Ah-in, Park Shin-hye
#Zombie #Apocalypse

□ **12.12: The Day 서울의 봄 2023 Historical, Drama / 141 min**
The tense chronicle of the 1979 Seoul coup d'état
Hwang Jung-min, Jung Woo-sung
#History #Coup #Politics

☐ **20th Century Girl 20세기 소녀 2022 Drama, Romance / 119 min**
In 1999, a teenage girl navigates friendship, heartbreak, and her first love.
Kim Yoo-jung, Byeon Woo-seok
#Coming-of-age #Friendship

■ **Aema 애마   2025 Historical, Comedy / 6 eps / TV-MA**
Actresses of 1980s erotic films confront censorship and hidden truths.
Lee Hanee, Bang Hyo-rin
#FemaleEmpowerment #Satire #1980s

■ **Alchemy of Souls 환혼**
2022-2023 Fantasy, Romance / 2 seasons
In a land of soul shifters, forbidden magic alters destinies and romance.
Lee Jae-wook, Jung So-min, Go Youn-jung
#Magic #Fantasy

☐ **Alienoid 외계+인 1, 2 2022 Sci-Fi, Action / 142 min, 122 min**
Aliens, time travel, and Joseon warriors collide in a chase across centuries.
Dir. Choi Dong-hoon, Kim Tae-ri, Kim Woo-bin
#TimeTravel #Joseon #Sci-Fi

■ **All of Us Are Dead 지금 우리 학교는**
2022 Horror, Thriller / 12 eps / TV-MA
A high school becomes ground zero of a zombie outbreak, trapping desperate students.
#Zombie #Survival #Webtoon

☐ **A Normal Family 보통의 가족 Disney+ 2024 Drama / 109 min**
A moral conflict unfolds between two brothers over their children.
Sul Kyung-gu, Jang Dong-gun
#MoralDilemma #Crime #PsychologicalTension #Family

■ A Shop for Killers 킬러들의 쇼핑몰
Disney+ 2024 Action, Crime / 8 eps / TV-MA

After her uncle's sudden death, a young heiress inherits his shop —and a deadly world of killers.
Lee Dong-wook, Kim Hye-jun
#Action #Crime #Webtoon

■ Beyond Evil 괴물   2021 Thriller, Crime / 16 eps

Two detectives hunt a serial killer while questioning if the real monster lies within themselves.
Shin Ha-kyun, Yeo Jin-goo
#Serial Killer #Mystery #Suspense

■ Big Bet 카지노
Disney+ 2022-2023 Drama / 2 seasons / TV-MA

A ruthless casino king and a relentless detective face off in Macau's high-stakes underworld.
Choi Min-sik, Son Suk-ku
#Casino #Crime #Power

■ Black Knight 택배기사   2023 Sci-Fi, Action / 6 eps

In a dystopian earth choked by pollution, a legendary deliveryman becomes humanity's lifeline.
Kim Woo-bin, Song Seung-heon
#Dystopia #Action #Survival

■ Blackout (Snow White Must Die) 블랙아웃
2020 Thriller / 14 eps

After years in prison, a man returns to his hometown, determined to uncover the dark truth behind the murder that shattered his life.
Dir. Byeon Young-Joo, Byun Yo-han
#FairyTale #Thriller #Novel

■ Bloodhounds 사냥개들   2023 Action, Thriller / 8 eps / TV-MA

Two rookie boxers plunge into the underworld to fight loan sharks for revenge.
Woo Do-hwan, Lee Sang-yi
#Boxing #LoanSharks #Action

■ Bon Appétit, Your Majesty 폭군의 셰프
2025 Time-Slip, Drama / 12 eps

A French chef time-slips into Joseon and must cook for
a tyrant king to survive.
Im Yoon-ah, Lee Chae-min
#Food #Drama #Fantasy #Romance

■ Business Proposal 사내맞선 2022 Romance, Comedy / 12 eps

A fake blind date spirals when she discovers
her boss is the match.
Ahn Hyo-seop, Kim Se-jeong
#FakeDating #Office #Webtoon

■ Can This Love Be Translated? 이 사랑 통역 되나요?
2025 Romance, Comedy/ TBD

Love gets lost—and found—in translation
Kim Seon-ho, Go Yoon-jung
#Translation #CelebrityRomance

■ Celebrity 셀러브리티 2023 Drama, Thriller / 12 eps / TV-MA

From nobody to social media stardom, a young woman is
dragged into a world of envy and scandal.
Park Kyu-young, Lee Cheong-ah
#InfluencerCulture #Scandal #Thriller

■ D.P. 2021-2023 Drama, Military / 2 seasons / TV-MA

In conscripted Korea, a sharp-eyed soldier joins the D.P. unit,
chasing deserters with stories of their own.
Jung Hae-in, Koo Kyo-hwan
#Army #Desertion #Drama

■ Daily Dose of Sunshine 정신병동에도 아침이 와요
2023 Drama, Medical / 12 eps

A psychiatric nurse confronts trauma and finds healing.
Park Bo-young, Yeon Woo-jin
#MentalHealth #Healing #Webtoon

☐ **Decision to Leave 헤어질 결심**
2022 Romance, Mystery / 138 min

A detective falls for a murder suspect, torn between love and suspicion.
Dir. Park Chan-wook, Tang Wei, Park Hae-il
#Mystery #Affair

■ **Diva on a Deserted Island 무인도의 디바**
2023 Drama, Romance / 12 eps

A singer stranded on an island survives alone and finally revives her long-delayed dream.
Park Eun-bin, Chae Jong-hyeop
#Music #Survival #Healing

■ **Doona! 이두나! 2023 Romance, Youth / 9 eps**

A former K-pop idol becomes a college student's housemate, setting off an unexpected journey of love and growth.
Bae Suzy, Yang Se-jong
#Romance #Sharehouse #IdolLife

■ **Eunjoong and Sangyeon 은중과 상연 2025 Drama / 15 eps**

Two ex-best friends reunite, bound by youth, loss, and longing.
Kim Go-eun, Park Ji-hyun
#Youth #Death #Friendship

■ **Extracurricular 인간수업 2020 Crime, Thriller / 10 eps / TV-MA**

A high schooler's side hustle spirals into a deadly crime.
Dir. Kim Jin-min, Kim Dong-hee, Park Ju-yeon
#Coming-of-age #Crime #Thriller

■ **Extraordinary Attorney Woo 이상한 변호사 우영우**
2022 Legal, Drama / 16 eps

A genius attorney with autism navigates a flawed yet warm world.
Park Eun-bin, Kang Tae-oh
#Autism #Law #Healing

■ **Fixer, The 형사록 1,2**
Disney+ 2022-2023 Crime, Thriller / 2 seasons
A veteran detective digs into cold cases with relentless resolve.
Lee Sung-min, Jin Goo
#Crime #Investigation #Thriller

■ **Glory, The 더 글로리 2022 Drama, Revenge / 16 eps / TV-MA**
Years after surviving brutal school bullying, a woman orchestrates
a chilling revenge against her tormentors.
Song Hye-kyo, Lim Ji-yeon
#Bullying #Revenge #Trauma

■ **Good Partner 굿파트너 2024 Drama, Legal / 16 eps**
A star divorce lawyer and a rookie face her own divorce
while teaming up.
Jang Na-ra, Nam Ji-hyun
#Law #Workplace #Rivalry

■ **Gyeongseong Creature 경성크리처**
2023-2024 Thriller, Historical, Fantasy / 2 seasons
In 1940s colonial Korea, survivors face unspeakable monsters
born of greed and oppression.
Park Seo-jun, Han So-hee
#Thriller #Historical #Creature #ColonialKorea

■ **Happiness 해피니스 2021 Thriller, Drama / 12 eps**
Residents in a high-rise face infection, fear, and survival under
lockdown.
Han Hyo-joo, Park Hyung-sik
#Infection #Survival

■ **Hellbound 지옥 2021, 2024 Fantasy, Thriller / 2 seasons**
When decrees of death are supernaturally delivered and executed,
society spirals into chaos.
Dir. Yeon Sang-ho, Yoo Ah-in
#Religion #Death #Supernatural

Hierarchy 하이라키 2024 Teen Drama, Mystery / 7 eps

A prestigious high school hides dark secrets behind its elite walls.
Roh Jeong-eui, Lee Chae-min
#Teen #Mystery #EliteSchool #Thriller

Hometown Cha-Cha-Cha 갯마을 차차차
2021 Romance, Slice of Life / 16 eps

In a seaside village, a city dentist and a local jack-of-all-trades find love and healing in community.
Shin Min-a, Kim Seon-ho
#SmallTown #Community #Healing

Hospital Playlist 슬기로운 의사생활 1,2
2020-2021 Drama, Medical / 2 seasons

Five longtime friends balance life as doctors, bandmates, and companions.
Jo Jung-suk, Yoo Yeon-seok
#Hospital #Friendship #Music

Hyena 하이에나 2020 Legal, Drama / 16 eps

Two fiery lawyers clash fiercely in court, blurring rivalry and romance.
Kim Hye-soo, Ju Ji-hoon
#Law #Rivalry

Hyperknife 하이퍼나이프
Disney+ 2025 Thriller, Action / 8 eps / TV-MA

A genius yet psychopathic doctor drives a razor-sharp medical thriller.
Park Eun-bin, Sul Kyung-gu
#Medical #Thriller #Action

Inspector Koo 구경이 2021 Thriller, DarkComedy / 12 eps

An eccentric detective faces off against a brilliant sociopathic killer in a darkly comic chase.
Lee Young-ae, Kim Hye-jun
#Investigation #DarkHumor #Mystery

■ **Itaewon Class 이태원 클라쓰 2020 Drama, Youth / 16 eps**
A high school dropout builds a restaurant empire in Itaewon, fueled by friendship and revenge.
Park Seo-joon, Kim Da-mi
#Entrepreneurship #Revenge #Webtoon

■ **Judge from Hell, The 지옥에서 온 판사**
Disney+ 2024 Fantasy, Drama 16 eps / TV-MA
When a devil inhabits the body of a principled judge, she joins forces with a human detective to deliver otherworldly justice on Earth.
Park Shin-hye, Kim Jae-young
#Fantasy #Crime #Supernatural

■ **Juvenile Justice 소년심판 2022 Legal, Drama / 10 eps / TV-MA**
A tough judge and a lenient colleague confront the brutal world of juvenile crime.
Kim Hye-soo, Kim Mu-yeol
#JuvenileCrime #Law #Justice

☐ **Kill Boksoon 길복순 2023 Action, Thriller / 137 min**
A mother who lives a double life as a contract killer struggles to balance family and survival.
Jeon Do-yeon, Sul Kyung-gu
#ContractKiller #Family #DualLife

■ **Killer's Paradox, The 살인자ㅇ난감**
2024 Comedy, Thriller / 8 eps / TV-MA
An accidental killer and the detective on his trail
Choi U-sik, Son Suk-ku
#Murder #Thriller

■ **Kingdom 킹덤 1, 2, Ashin of the North 2019-2021 Historical, Zombie / 2 seasons & a special episode / TV-MA**
In Joseon Korea, a crown prince battles a deadly plague that turns people into the undead.
Ju Ji-hoon, Bae Doona
#Zombie #Joseon #Power

■ **King's Affection, The 연모 2021 Historical, Romance / 20 eps**
A woman who takes her twin brother's place on the throne hides her secret while falling in love.
Park Eun-bin, Rowoon
#Joseon #Cross-dressing #Romance

■ **Korea-Khitan War, The 고려 거란 전쟁**
2023 Historical, War / 32 eps
Goryeo resists the Khitan invasion with loyalty and sacrifice.
Kim Dong-jun, Choi Su-jong
#Goryeo #KhitanInvasion #Loyalty

■ **Law School 로스쿨 2021 Legal, Drama / 16 eps**
A professor and his student, solving crimes through lessons
Kim Myung-min, Ryu Hae-young
#Crime #Thriller #Persona #Growth

■ **Little Women 작은 아씨들 2022 Drama, Mystery / 12 eps**
Three sisters become entangled in a conspiracy against Korea's richest and most powerful.
Kim Go-eun, Chu Ja-hyun
#Family #Conspiracy #Mystery

■ **Love Alarm 좋아하면 울리는**
2019-2021 Romance, Drama / 2 Seasons
An app alerts you when someone nearby likes you.
Kim So-hyun, Song Kang
#Technology #FirstLove #High School

■ **Love and Leashes 모럴센스 2022 Romance, Comedy / 117 min**
An office romance with a kinky twist
Seohyun, Lee Jun-young
#Office #Romance #Kink #Webtoon

☐ **Love in the Big City 대도시의 사랑법**
2024 Romance, LGBTQ+ / 118 min
Queer love stories set in modern Seoul
Kim Go-eun, Noh Sang-hyun
#Queer #Seoul #Adaptation

■ **Lovely Runner 선재 업고 튀어**
2024 Time-slip, Romance / 16 eps
A fan travels back in time to save her idol from a tragic fate.
Byeon Woo-seok, Kim Hye-yoon
#Time-travel #Redemption #Music

■ **Mantis 사마귀   2025 Action, Thriller / 8 eps**
A detective discovers that his mother, a notorious serial killer, may
hold the key to a new string of murders.
Dir. Byun Young-joo, Go Hyung-jeong
#Spin-off #Action #Thriller

■ **Mask Girl 마스크걸   2023 Thriller, Drama / 7 eps / TV-MA**
A masked life spirals into crime and revenge.
Go Hyun-jung, Nana
#Webtoon #Identity #Revenge

□ **Minari 미나리   2021 Drama / 115 min**
A Korean American family struggles to put down roots like minari .
Dir. Lee Isaac Chung, Steven Yeun, Han Ye-ri
#Immigration #Family #Hope

■ **Missing: The Other Side 미씽 1, 2**
2020-2022 Fantasy, Mystery / 2 Seasons
A mediator between life and death uncovers the secrets of the
missing.
Go Soo, Heo Joon-ho
#MissingPeople #Afterlife #Mystery

■ **Move to Heaven 무브 투 헤븐   2021 Drama / 10 eps**
A trauma cleaner tells the stories left behind.
Lee Je-hoon, Tang Jun-sang
#TraumaCleaner #Healing #Family

■ **Moving 무빙   Disney+ 2023 Action, Fantasy / 20 eps**
Across generations, superpowered heroes unite and fight.
Ryu Seung-ryong, Han Hyo-joo
#Superpower #Heroes #Family

■ **Mr. Plankton Mr. 플랑크톤 2024 Romantic Comedy / 10 eps**
An unhappy bride joins a dying man on his last journey.
Woo Do-hwan, Lee Yoo-mi
#BlackComedy #Growth #Romance

■ **Mr. Queen 철인왕후 2020 Historical, Comedy / 20 eps**
A modern-day chef time-slips into the queen's body.
Shin Hye-sun, Kim Jung-hyun
#Joseon #Body-Swap #Comedy #Time-slip

■ **My Demon 마이 디몬 2023 Romance, Fantasy / 16 eps**
A devilish heiress and a powerless demon enter a contract
marriage for salvation.
Kim Yoo-jung, Song Kang
#Romance #Fantasy #ContractMarriage #Supernatural

■ **My Liberation Notes 나의 해방일지**
2022 Drama, Slice of Life / 16 eps
Three siblings long to escape their stifling lives and find liberation.
Lee Min-gi, Kim Ji-won, Son Suk-ku
#Family #Escape #Love

■ **My Name 마이 네임 2021 Action, Thriller / 8 eps / TV-MA**
To avenge her father, a woman goes undercover in a crime
syndicate.
Dir. Kim Jin-min, Han So-hee, Park Hee-soon
#Revenge #Crime #Undercover #Action

■ **Narco-Saints 수리남 2022 Crime, Thriller / 6 eps / TV-MA**
An ordinary man is drawn into a mission to bring down
Suriname's drug cartel.
Ha Jung-woo, Hwang Jung-min
#Drugs #Crime #Survival

■ **Navillera 나빌레라 2021 Drama, Slice of Life / 12 eps**
A 70-year-old pursues ballet, joining forces with a drifting young
dancer.
Park In-hwan, Song Kang
#Dreams #Ageing #Friendship

☐ **Night in Paradise 낙원의 밤 2021 Crime, Noir / 131 min**
Two lost souls spend their final days on the edge of violence.
Uhm Tae-goo, Jeon Yeo-been
#Revenge #Violence #Gangsters

◼ **Our Beloved Summer 그해 우리는**
2021 Romance, Drama / 16 eps
A youthful romance rekindled as former lovers reunite
Choi Woo-shik, Kim Da-mi
#Youth #Love #Documentary

◼ **Our Blues 우리들의 블루스 2022 Drama, Slice of Life / 20 eps**
Interwoven stories of love, family, and friendship set in Jeju
Lee Byung-hun, Shin Min-a, Kim Hye-ja
#Jeju #Community #Healing

◼ **Pachinko 파친코 1, 2**
Apple TV+ 2022-2024 Drama, Historical / 2 Seasons
The four-generation saga of a Korean family living in Japan
Youn Yuh-jung, Kim Min-ha, Lee Min-ho
#Zainichi #Family #History

◼ **Parasyte: The Grey 기생수: 더 그레이**
2024 Sci-Fi, Horror, Action / 6 eps
As humans battle alien parasites, one girl struggles to survive
as their host.
Jeon So-nee, Koo Kyo-hwan
#Sci-Fi #Horror #WebtoonAdaptation

◼ **Queen of Tears 눈물의 여왕 2024 Romance, Drama / 16 eps**
A chaebol heiress and her lawyer husband face crisis,
rediscovering love in marriage.
Kim Soo-hyun, Kim Ji-won
#Chaebol #Marriage #Healing

◼ **Reborn Rich 재벌집 막내아들 2022 Fantasy, Drama / 16 eps**
A risk manager is reborn as a chaebol heir and plots revenge
with a second life.
Song Joong-ki, Lee Sung-min
#Chaebol #Rebirth #Revenge

■ **Red Sleeve, The 옷소매 붉은 끝동**
2021 Historical, Romance / 17 eps

A king and his court lady share a poignant love within
the palace walls.
Lee Jun-ho, Lee Se-young
#Joseon #Palace #Romance

■ **Resident Playbook 언젠가는 슬기로운 전공의생활**
2025 Drama, Medical / 12 eps

In the Hospital Playlist world, residents struggle through trials of
love and growth.
Go Youn-jung, Shin Si-a, Kang You-seok
#Hospital #SliceOfLife #Growth

■ **Revenant 악귀 Disney+ 2023**
Drama, Occult Thriller 12 eps TV-MA

A woman possessed by an evil spirit and a folklorist who can
see ghosts uncover a chain of mysterious deaths tied to ancient
curses.
Kim Tae-ri, Oh Jung-se
#Occult #Supernatural #Folklore

■ **School Nurse Files, The 보건교사 안은영**
2020 Fantasy, Comedy / 6 eps

A ghost-hunting school nurse confronts strange mysteries only
she can see.
Jung Yu-mi, Nam Joo-hyuk
#School #Fantasy #Healing

■ **Silent Sea, The 고요의 바다 2021 Sci-Fi, Thriller / 8 eps**

On a deserted lunar base, a crew faces deadly mysteries in
a survival mission.
Bae Doona, Gong Yoo
#Space #Mystery #Apocalypse

■ **Sound of Magic, The 안나라수마나라**
2022 Fantasy, Musical / 6 eps

A mysterious magician and a lonely girl share moments
that could change their world.
Ji Chang-wook, Choi Sung-eun
#Magic #ChildhoodTrauma #Musical #Webtoon

■ **Squid Game 오징어게임 1, 2, 3**
2021-2025 Thriller, Survival / 3 seasons / TV-MA

In a mysterious survival game, desperate contestants stake their lives for fortune.
Lee Jung-jae, Park Hae-soo, Lee Byung-hun
#Survival #Game #Dystopia

■ **Stranger (Secret Forest) 비밀의 숲 1,2**
2017-2020 Thriller, Crime / 16 eps each

A cold prosecutor and a warm-hearted detective uncover crime and corruption.
Cho Seung-woo, Bae Doona
#Crime #Corruption #Mystery

■ **Sweet Home 스위트홈**
2020-2023 Horror, Thriller / 3 seasons / TV-MA

Trapped in an apocalyptic apartment, survivors battle monsters—and their own humanity.
Song Kang, Lee Jin-uk
#Creature #Disaster #Dystopia

■ **Takryu 탁류**
Disney+ 2025 Historical, Action Drama / 16 eps / TV-MA

Set against the turbulence of Joseon, three people with hidden pasts struggle for survival and justice.
Nam Joo-hyuk, Park Hye-su
#Historical #Action #Survival

■ **Tastefully Yours 당신의 맛 2025 Romance, Drama / 10 eps**

A recipe-hunting chaebol and a master chef share a slow-cooked romance of healing.
Kang Ha-neul, Go Min-si
#Food #Romance #Healing

■ **Taxi Driver 모범택시 1,2,3 2021-2025 Action, Crime / 3 seasons**

A secret taxi service avenges the powerless, delivering justice outside the law.
Lee Je-hoon, Esom
#Revenge #Crime #Justice

■ **Through the Darkness 악의 마음을 읽는 자들**
2022 Thriller, Crime / 12 eps

Korea's first criminal profiler enters the dark minds of
serial killers.
Kim Nam-gil, Jin Seon-kyu
#Profiler #SerialKillers

☐ **Time to Hunt 사냥의 시간   2020 Thriller, Sci-Fi | 134 min**

In a dystopian city, young ex-cons risk everything on a desperate
heist for freedom.
Lee Je-hoon, Choi Woo-shik
#Dystopia #Heist #Survival

■ **Trauma Code: Heroes on Call, The 중증외상센터**
2025 Medical, Drama / 8 eps

When a genius surgeon joins a failing trauma team, Korea's ER
battle begins.
Ju Ji-hoon, Chu Young-woo, Ha Young
#Hospital #Emergency

■ **Trigger 트리거   2025 Thriller, Action / 10 eps / TV-MA**

In gun-free Korea, the sudden influx of firearms ignites a deadly
crisis.
Kim Nam-gil, Kim Young-kwang
#Crime #Thriller #Action

■ **True Beauty 여신강림   2020 Romance, Youth / 16 eps**

A high school girl hides behind makeup, but love threatens to
reveal her true self.
Moon Ga-young, Cha Eun-woo, Hwang In-yeop
#WebtoonAdaptation #Romance #HighSchool

■ **Twenty-Five Twenty-One 스물다섯 스물하나**
2022 Romance, Drama / 16 eps

In an era of uncertainty, young fencers pursue dreams, love, and
bittersweet growth.
Kim Tae-ri, Nam Joo-hyuk
#Youth #Sports #Nostalgia

■ **Typhoon Company 태풍상사 2025 Drama / 16 eps**

Set in 1997 amid Korea's IMF crisis, it follows rookie salesman-turned CEO Kang Tae-poong-whose name means "typhoon"-as he fights to save his late father's bankrupt trading company.
Lee Junho, Kim Min-ha
#Drama #Retro #Growth

■ **Under the Queen's Umbrella 슈룰**
2022 Historical, Drama / 16 eps

In Joseon's palace, a fierce queen fights to protect her sons amid an education war.
Kim Hye-soo, Kim Hae-sook
#Joseon #Motherhood #Palace

■ **Unknown Seoul 미지의 서울 2025 Drama / 12 eps**

Twin sisters trade lives, uncovering identity, love, and family along the way.
Park Bo-young, Park Jin-young
#Identity #Family #Urban

☐ **Unlocked 스마트폰을 떨어뜨렸을 뿐인데 2023 Thriller / 117 min**

Losing a smartphone spirals into a nightmare of privacy invasion and crime.
Chun Woo-hee, Im Si-wan
#Technology #Thriller #Crime

■ **Vincenzo 빈센조 2021 Dark Comedy, Crime, Romance / 20 eps**

A Korean-Italian mafia lawyer delivers his own style of justice.
Song Joong-ki, Jeon Yeo-been, Ok Taec-yeon
#DarkComedy #Mafia #Antihero #Action

■ **Weak Hero Class 1,2 약한영웅**
2022, 2025 Action, Youth / 2 seasons / TV-MA

Behind his frail appearance, a brilliant but brutal fighter rises against bullies in a violent world.
Park Ji-hoon, Choi Hyun-wook
#Bullying #Coming-of-age #Action

■ When Life Gives You Tangerines 폭싹 속았수다
2025 Drama, Romance / 16 eps

Through a Jeju couple and their families, a timeless love story unfolds.
IU, Park Bo-gum
#Jeju #LifeStory

■ When the Phone Rings 지금 거신 전화는
2024 Drama, Thriller / 12 eps

An arranged marriage turns perilous as suspense deepens and unexpected love emerges.
Yoo Yeon-suk, Chae Su-bin
#Thriller #Suspense #Romance

■ World of the Married, The 부부의 세계
2020 Drama, Romance, Thriller / 16 eps / TV-MA

A respected doctor's picture-perfect life shatters when she discovers her husband's betrayal, spiraling into obsession, revenge, and raw emotional warfare. Adaption of the BBC drama 'Doctor Foster'.
Kim Hee-ae, Park Hae-joon, Han So-hee
#Drama #Romance #Thriller

■ Worst Evil, The 최악의 악
Disney+ 2023 Crime, Action Thriller / 12 eps / TV-MA

A rural detective infiltrates a powerful crime syndicate in Gangnam, torn between ambition, loyalty, and the woman he loves.
Ji Chang-wook, Wi Ha-joon
#Crime #Thriller #Undercover

■ Youth of May 오월의 청춘 2021 Historical, Romance / 12 eps

Amid the 1980 Gwangju uprising, two young lovers are swept into history's storm.
Lee Do-hyun, Go Min-si
#Gwangju #Democracy #Youth

And that was our playlist from Korea – 101 recent picks from 2020 onward. A playlist to guide your first steps through the Land of K – there's much more to discover beyond.

Extra Goodies

Visit

oksusupie.kr to download digital files from the bonus chapters and more.

Includes:

- Hangeul Consonant & Vowel Chart
- 101 Titles from 2020 Onward

Coming Next from OksusuPie

(Titles and publishing order subject to change)

▌Your Binge List for the Holidays!

A Chill Guide Annex Edition featuring 500+ picks & rich stories from the world of K-content - curated for binge-watchers and culture lovers alike, with hidden gems waiting to be found.

▌OKsusu Korean: A Hangeul Primer
From Sounds to Sentences

A real beginner's guide to Hangeul, the Korean Alphabet. Master how each sound works together - from simple syllables to real Korean words and sentences.

▌A Chill Guide to Korean Jindo

From royal legends to modern-day companions, explore Korea's beloved Jindo dogs and the country's unique culture of canine companionship.

▌Text & Illustration by **Ihm Minyong**

A native Korean who spent half a lifetime in Seoul and
seven years wandering through California and Washington.

Now tucked away in a quiet mountain town at the heart of Korea,
Ihm enjoys reading, writing, and reflecting on all things K-
both online and off.

Drawing on a background in literature and Korean language education,
Ihm is dedicated to creative publishing and storytelling
that illuminate the many layers of Korean culture.

www.ingramcontent.com/pod-product-compliance
Lightning Source LLC
Chambersburg PA
CBHW052020030426
42335CB00026B/3228